CH00802656

Text by Lara Belonogoff
Photography by Anna Mockford and Nick Bonetti
Edited by Alex Knights and John Mapps
Series Editor: Tony Halliday

Berlitz® POCKET GUIDE

Vilnius

First Edition 2005

PHOTOGRAPHY CREDITS

All photography (including cover) by Anna Mockford and Nick Bonetti, except page 92 by Jon Smith.

CONTACTING THE EDITORS

Every effort has been made to provide accurate information in this publication, but changes are inevitable. The publisher cannot be responsible for any resulting loss, inconvenience or injury. We would appreciate it if readers would call our attention to any errors or outdated information by contacting Berlitz Publishing, PO Box 7910, London SE1 1WE, England.
Fax: (44) 20 7403 0290;
e-mail: berlitz@apaguide.co.uk
www.berlitzpublishing.com

► Explore the richly historic streets of the Old Town of Kaunas (page 72), the second-largest city in Lithuania

Religion and history meet at the Gates of Dawn (page 34), a pilgrimage site built into a medieval city gate ▲

Gediminas Tower (page 31) affords one of the best views in town ▼

TOP TEN ATTRACTIONS

Wander through the ornate courtyards of Vilnius University (page 43) ▼

◄ Historic Vilnius Cathedral (page 27) is the city's most important building

One of the symbols of Vilnius, ► St Anne's Church (page 56) is noted for its elaborate brick facade

The restored medieval Trakai Castle (page 65) is as impressive today as it was when first built ▼

► Sculpture from around the world distinguishes Europe's Park (page 67)

Lithuanian bohemia: the arty Užupis district (page 57) ►

Lakes and pine forests dominate Aukštaitija National Park (page 76), northeast of Vilnius ►

CONTENTS

Fact Sheets

INTRODUCTION

Vilnius' Old Town preserves a rich architectural legacy, with baroque and Gothic dominating, but also including most other major European styles, especially Renaissance and neoclassical. Inside a building like the Church of Sts Peter and Paul, the flamboyant scale of the baroque decoration can be almost overwhelming. On the streets, little details such as richly ornamented plasterwork, wrought-iron shop signs and secluded courtyards catch the eye. Every other cobbled lane seems to lead towards the steeple of a Catholic church or the cupola of an Orthodox one. There are more than 1,500 historic buildings, and the entire Old Town is classified as a World Heritage Site.

Lithuanian handicraft

That this legacy has been preserved is nothing short of miraculous, given Lithuania's often turbulent history, particularly in the 20th century. The 1991 re-establishment of independence saw Vilnius smarten itself up, renovating its Old Town treasures, and opening new restaurants, cafés, bars and hotels. The city has thrown open its arms to foreign visitors, yet mass tourism has not taken hold, making Vilnius a refreshing change from some of Europe's more touristy destinations. Lithuanians as a whole are welcoming to foreigners (although a service culture is yet to take root), and English is widely understood.

A Lithuanian folk dancer from Pamusis

The large egg in a nest on Plačioji Street was originally located where the Užupis angel now stands *(see page 60)*. At first there was just a plinth, then the egg was erected on top to show that plans for the Angel would soon hatch. After the statue had been put up, city officials decided to relocate the egg and provide a nest for it. There are plans to move the egg to areas of town that are being reconstructed or updated.

Part of Vilnius' appeal is its fascinating mixture of people. This city of 540,000 has long been a multicultural place. A 15-minute walk through the Old Town provides a crash-course in northeastern European languages. Even though some 80 percent of the national population is ethnic Lithuanian, in the capital there are significant numbers of Poles, Belarussians and Russians, as well as a small Jewish population, a mere shadow, sadly, of the vibrant prewar Jewish community that earned Vilnius the nickname 'Jerusalem of the North'.

In the relatively short summer, when the sun rises early and sets late, the people of Vilnius spend as much time as possible each day outside, thronging the city's streets, parks and café terraces. Cooler weather tempers the outdoor spirit but works wonders for the city's plants and trees, especially in autumn when the many deciduous trees turn shades of red and gold. Winters are long and hard, and Vilnius' people switch to indoor pursuits. Intrepid travellers might consider a visit over the Christmas–New Year period to see how snow and ice transform the alleys and squares of the Old Town into a scene from a fairytale.

World Heritage Site

The Old Town struggled through the Soviet era, its churches turned into warehouses or museums, its houses becoming steadily more dilapidated, and its residents enduring a primitive sewerage system and shortage of hot water. When the Republic of Lithuania was re-established, fixing up the shabby Old Town was one of the first orders of business. Churches were returned to their religious communities, and private property returned to its original owners. But the fledgling government had little money to spare on renovation projects. Fortunately, the 1994 UNESCO listing of the Old Town as a World Heritage Site ensured a faster flow of funds. Revitalisation of the Old Town began in earnest the following year and continues to this day. Nearly US$17 million of municipal and state funds, and about four times that amount from private sources, have been spent to great effect – street lamps are working, streets are paved, squares and parks have been preserved and buildings have been painted muted hues of yellow, orange and pink.

The egg on Plačioji Street is a symbol of the city's revitalisation

Bustling Cathedral Square

For a glimpse of what Vilnius was like just a few decades ago, look past the spruced-up exteriors into some of the city's courtyards, many of which are very shabby indeed. Although privatisation took place, many flat owners did not own the land around them and there was no incentive for them to clear up their courtyards. Home-owner associations, still being set up, are taking care of this problem, and they promise to beautify every nook of the city over time.

Modernisation and its Consequences

The Old Town is not the only part of Vilnius in the process of transformation. The changing face of the city and its propulsion into a new phase is illustrated by the amount of construction taking place. For instance, the district of Šnipiškės, lying just across the Neris River from the centre of town, has undergone massive changes in recent times. Old wooden one-, two- and three-storey houses were always more common here than concrete Soviet housing blocks, but the area is now being developed into a modern business district. Scaffolding still surrounds many of the area's projects, and residents may soon have to decide whether to cash in and leave with the profits from the increased value of their properties stuffed in their pockets, or remain among the new buildings. Property prices are also on the up in the bohemian district of Užupis, haunt of artists, musicians and eccentrics, as the newly wealthy flood into the area. How this trend will end is anyone's guess.

Renovation of the Old Town and the development of new business areas apart, the central portions of the city have also tried to revitalise themselves in a post-Communist world. The nascent tourism industry is constantly finding new ways to lure visitors, while businesses in general are trying to encourage more of the population to use their services. Not all entrepreneurs have cultural revitalisation as one of their goals. A considerable number of strip clubs have opened throughout the city since the mid-1990s, and Vilnius is starting to be marketed in some European countries as a venue for stag parties. Furthermore, the legalisation of gambling in 2001 has brought a handful of casinos to the main streets. Flashing neon lights and pictures of scantily clad women are now more prominent in a city whose real charm lies in its well-preserved medieval and baroque roots.

Historic Dominukonų Street in the Old Town *(see page 41)*

Cultural and National Identity

The chapel in the Gates of Dawn is a renowned pilgrimage site

Throughout the tumultuous history of Vilnius, during which sovereignty and property changed hands several times and even street names were altered to reflect the current ruling group's ideology, there were certain things that anchored the citizens to a national identity. Many of the country's writers, thinkers, poets, philosophers and graphic artists have concerned themselves with the question of what this identity actually is. To answer it, they looked for something they considered authentically 'Lithuanian' or unspoilt within their own history and culture.

One of the things they focused on was the Lithuanian language. Linguistically, its only close relatives are Latvian and Sanskrit. The use of the language in itself ensured that Polish or Russian influence was for the most part minimal. The second fortress of a purely Lithuanian identity was found in the country's folklore and traditional pagan beliefs. As the last people in Europe to convert to Christianity, Lithuanians managed to keep many of their nature-based traditions alive.

The mining of folklore and other beliefs for stories in order to produce works distinctly Lithuanian continues to this day in both high- and low-brow art worlds. A great number of the artworks being produced by the country's city-dwelling young people integrate the natural world and Lithuanian folklore. This, coupled with the many festivals that have more than just a pagan aura, ensure that ancient traditions are not extinguished and that a distinctive Lithuanian identity continues.

A BRIEF HISTORY

Legend credits the founding of Vilnius to Gediminas, Grand Duke of Lithuania (1316–41). One day, so the story goes, Gediminas was hunting in the Šventaragis Valley at the foot of present-day Gediminas Hill. Falling asleep, he dreamt of an iron wolf that howled with the ferocity of 100 wolves. One of his pagan high priests interpreted the dream to mean that a city was to be built where Gediminas had rested and, moreover, that this city would become unconquerable and as resilient as an iron wolf. The howl signified the strength of the city's voice in the world.

Grand Duke Gediminas, founder of Vilnius, in Cathedral Square

A Capital Emerges

Archaeological evidence tells a more prosaic story. There has been a settlement at the confluence of the Neris and Vilnia rivers since around 2000–2500BC. By 500BC a substantial community lived at the foot of Gediminas Hill. About AD1000 a wooden castle was built on top of the hill.

Mindaugas is the first Lithuanian ruler we know much about. In the mid-14th century he united various tribal chieftains and converted to Christianity (the country was still largely pagan) in an attempt to impress Europe's Christian states. He was crowned first king of Lithuania on 6 July 1253, but was murdered 10 years later by pagan nobles. During his reign Vilnius Cathedral was built.

Gediminas emerged in the early 14th century as a far-sighted and powerful ruler. He wrote to numerous German towns inviting their merchants, craftsmen and priests to settle in Vilnius. Although most of the country was still pagan, Gediminas offered those willing to move to Vilnius the autonomy to practise their own religion. This tolerance became one of the ideological foundations of the city. In order to ensure peace, Gediminas signed a treaty with the port-city of Riga, in neighbouring Latvia, in 1323 and in 1325 formed a union with Poland by marrying off his daughter Aldona to the Polish king's son.

Pagan Lithuania had become a target for crusading religious orders, especially the Teutonic Knights, who invaded the country several times in the late 14th century. Preventing these attacks proved impossible for Gediminas. He moved the capital 28km (17 miles) to the east from his castle at Trakai to a newly built castle on Gediminas Hill, perhaps because Vilnius could be defended more easily from there. When Vilnius next found itself under attack by the Teutonic Knights, most of the wooden city burned, but the crusaders were unable to seize the stone Higher Castle.

When Jogaila became king of both Poland and Lithuania, his cousin, Vytautas, was given the new king's previous position as Grand Prince of Lithuania. It was Vytautas, later Grand Duke, who was responsible for the building of the red-brick castle at Trakai after the nearby castle of his father, Kęstutis, had been attacked once too often by German crusaders.

Teutonic Knights defeated at Grünwald, or Tannenberg

After Gediminas' death, the Lithuanian state fell into disarray, as two of his grandsons, Vytautas and Jogaila, fought for power. Jogaila eventually came to an agreement with Vytautas, and in 1387 signed the Treaty of Kréva (or Krewo), whereby he agreed to marry the Polish Princess Jadwiga and become king of Poland. He moved to Kraków after converting to Christianity and re-establishing a bishopric and the cathedral in Vilnius. This marriage was the beginning of the long-standing Polish–Lithuanian Commonwealth, in which Lithuania was an autonomous Grand Duchy.

On 15 July 1410, at the battle of Grünwald or Žalgiris (also referred to as Tannenberg), a coalition of Polish and Lithuanian forces defeated the Teutonic Knights. The battle dealt a crushing blow to the belligerent order, and meant that Vilnius could flourish in peace. The town expanded and took on a multi-ethnic character, its population including Lithuanians, Poles, Germans, Jews and even Tatars.

Building a City

After the death of Jogaila (in Poland referred to as Jagiełło) in 1434, his descendants continued to rule the Commonwealth. Casimir Jageillon (1440–92, father of St Casimir), Alexander Jageillon (1492–1506), Sigismund the Old (1506–48) and Sigismund Augustus (1548–72) all left evidence of their rule in Vilnius. Casimir was instrumental in replacing the city's wooden structures with brick buildings, thereby making the city more formidable to its enemies. During Alexander's time nearly 20 guilds were established, giving Vilnius a name for its craftsmen. He also began the construction of a wall, meant to surround and protect the city from attacks by Tatars. Bona Sforza, the Italian princess who married Sigismund the Old, helped spread the ideas and tastes of the Italian Renaissance. One of Sigismund Augustus' projects was rebuilding the Lower Castle, burned in a 1503 fire, and turning it into a

Detail from a brass door in Vilnius University

salon for the gentry. The re-building served to cultivate a rebirth of arts and culture. The late 16th century saw the introduction of the baroque style to Vilnius.

The death of Sigismund Augustus brought an end to the Jogaila (Jagiełło) dynasty. Lithuania was drawn closer to Poland politically and culturally. Polish had replaced Lithuanian among nobles by the 16th century.

The Artillery Bastion dates from the 17th century

Changing Hands

Conflict with Sweden and Russia grew over the next century or so. During the Great Northern War (1700–21), both Swedish and Russian forces tried to invade Vilnius. The Russians began to chip away at the foundations of the Polish–Lithuanian Commonwealth itself, and in 1795, they formally absorbed the Grand Duchy of Lithuania.

An uprising against the Russian Empire in 1831 resulted, the following year, in the closing of Vilnius University, where some staff and students had organised protests. The state of Lithuania was erased from maps and became known as the Northwest Region. The country was also subjected to Russification; the Lithuanian language could be written only in Cyrillic letters and many non-Orthodox churches were closed. In 1863 another uprising resulted in the hanging of leading activists in Lukiškių Square at the hands of General Muryavov, nicknamed 'the Hangman'. Lithuanian nationalism went underground.

The early part of World War I saw a succession of German victories against Russia. On 18 September 1915, the German army seized Vilnius, intending to keep Lithuania as a kind of satellite state. But the 1917 Russian Revolution emboldened Lithuanian nationalists, and on 16 February 1918 the 20-member association of the elected Lithuanian Council in Vilnius broke off relations with all other countries and declared its independence. German troops began to withdraw. The newly independent Lithuania was still wet behind the ears as first Pol-

Napoleon's Frozen Grand Army

The Žirmūnai suburb adjacent to Antakalnis was the focus of historical debate in early 2001, when workers from a housing development stumbled on what was at first believed to be a mass grave of victims of the Soviet regime. However, as the remains were sifted, it became clear from coins and fragments of army uniforms that the bodies were soldiers from Napoleon's Grand Army.

Numbering nearly half a million in its prime, the army was the largest ever raised in Europe. In June 1812, they marched through Vilnius on the way to Moscow and were welcomed by the city's residents as liberators from the Russian occupation. Five months later, the defeated army numbered a mere 40,000. Trailing back to Paris, the wounded and starving soldiers arrived in Vilnius in freezing temperatures of around −30°C (−22°F). That winter a further 30,000 died. With corpses littering the streets, the citizens of Vilnius tried – and failed – to come up with a solution of how to dispose of the bodies. Eventually, as Russian forces reoccupied the city, the dead were placed in the thawed ground of a trench dug by the French Army on their advance to Moscow. They had dug their own graves.

Another trench, with nearly 20,000 skeletons, was unearthed a few months after the initial find. The bones were placed in the sanctuary of Antakalnis cemetery and are commemorated with a statue.

ish then Soviet armies attacked and occupied the city.

Poland wished to reincorporate Lithuania. Its forces, under Józef Piłsudski, occupied the city and the region around it from 1920 to 1939. They renamed this area Middle Lithuania, claiming the state as a former territory of the Polish–Lithuanian Commonwealth. Kaunas, the second-largest city in Lithuania, served as the interim capital for the part of the Lithuanian state remaining independent.

The grave of Józef Piłsudski in Rasų Cemetery *(see page 62)*

Soviet Lithuania

On 23 August 1939, Hitler and Stalin signed the secret Molotov–Ribbentrop Pact, which divided Europe between Germany and the USSR. The Baltic states came within the Soviet Union's agreed sphere of influence. By 18 September, just over two weeks after the start of World War II, Vilnius was occupied by the Soviets, who promptly ceded the city back to the Lithuanian state. On 26 October the Lithuanian Army marched into Vilnius, but by the following summer Soviet soldiers, ostensibly stationed to protect against possible invading German forces, had control of the entire city. Many of Vilnius' citizens were deported to labour camps in Siberia or executed.

It was not entirely surprising that when the Germans occupied Vilnius at the end of June 1941 many of the city's residents hoped that they would alleviate the problems of Soviet domination. Events proved them tragically wrong.

National heroes, Steponas Darius and Stasys Girėnas died in an attempt to fly from New York to Kaunas in 1932 *(see page 73)*

About 42,000 Jews were placed in the Vilnius ghetto; most of them were then murdered in mass executions in Paneriai, about 8km (5 miles) outside Vilnius. The Jewish population of the city was almost entirely destroyed.

The Soviet Army advanced into Lithuania in 1944, occupying Vilnius on 13 July. A reign of terror followed. People were deported, tortured, executed or simply went missing. After Stalin's demise in 1953 the death toll decreased but did not cease. More emphasis was now placed on ideological control, but even with the enormous weight of the Soviet system Vilnius managed to maintain a rich cultural heritage and a respected arts scene led by painters, filmmakers and jazz musicians. The city also managed to retain most of its baroque architecture and the layout of the Old Town was kept in its medieval form. The only area of the Old Town to suffer significant damage was the Jewish Quarter.

Independence

In the mid-1980s, the new Soviet leader, Mikhail Gorbachev, embarked on a policy of reform and greater openness that had the unintended effect of encouraging independence movements throughout the Soviet bloc. In 1986 the Lithuanian press put forward the idea of restoring the pre-Soviet names of streets, a small move that many see as the beginning of the unravelling of the Soviet grip on the country. Sąjūdis, a pro-independence group, was formed in 1988. A year later, Sąjūdis help organise a massive popular protest: a human chain linking Vilnius, Riga (Latvia) and Tallinn (Estonia) to commemorate the 50th anniversary of the Molotov–Ribbentrop Pact. Nearly 2 million people joined hands to cross the 650km (400-mile) distance. On 11 March 1990, the Supreme Council of Lithuania (the future Seimas, or parliament) demanded the withdrawal of Soviet forces and an independent Lithuanian state.

On 13 January 1991 Soviet authorities tried to storm the parliamentary building (where Sąjūdis members had already won 106 out of the 141 seats of the Soviet Lithuanian Republic) and the Vilnius Television Tower. Large crowds surrounded the parliamentary building and the Soviets did not attack, but 14 civilians were killed in a clash at the Television Tower. The Soviets maintained nominal control over Lithuania until the failure of the August 1991 coup against Gorbachev. Lithuania was now truly independent, and the last Soviet

Memorial for victims of the Jewish genocide *(see page 53)*

troops left two years later. Within a year Lithuania joined NATO's Partnership for Peace and Vilnius' Old Town made it onto the UNESCO World Heritage list. Lithuania became a full-fledged member of NATO in the spring of 2004.

Membership of the European Union was a crucial goal. On 12 June 1995 Lithuania signed an Association Agreement with the EU, but had to negotiate several stumbling blocks to gain EU accession, including capital punishment and the future of the Chernobyl-style Ignalina nuclear power plant, about 100km (62 miles) northeast of Vilnius. Lithuania abolished the death penalty in 1998, but the reactor problem proved much more difficult. Although Swedish officials stepped in shortly after independence to try to ensure that the plant was safe, many EU members wished to see the reactor, which provides almost all Lithuania's energy, closed. Finally, the government agreed to decommission the reactor by around 2015. On 1 May 2004, with the Lithuanian currency, the lita, pegged to the euro, Lithuania became an EU member.

With democracy came some corruption. The first large-scale scandal in the government surfaced in 2003 when newly elected President Rolandas Paksas, a former mayor of Vilnius, was alleged to have been involved in less-than-legal campaign funding and to have associated with unsavoury Russian 'businessmen'. Paksas was ousted from office in June 2004 and replaced by 77-year-old Valdas Adamkus, an émigré from the United States who had already acted as president of the republic from 1998 to 2003.

Election poster

Historical Landmarks

700BC The first Baltic tribes settle in present-day Lithuania and Latvia.

1253 Duke Mindaugas is crowned Lithuania's king.

1323 Vilnius is officially founded by Grand Duke Gediminas.

1387 Gediminas' grandson, Jogaila, signs the Kréva or Krewo Union, creating the Polish–Lithuanian Commonwealth.

1410 Joint Polish–Lithuanian forces led by Jogaila and his cousin Vytautas defeat the Teutonic Knights.

1430 The Commonwealth extends from the Baltic to the Black Sea. Grand Duke Vytautas dies without an heir. The Polish increase their influence in Lithuania.

1572 Jogaila dynasty ends; Lithuania's role in Commonwealth is marginalised.

1700s Vilnius is attacked by Swedish and Russian forces.

1795 Lithuania becomes part of Russia.

1812 Napoleon's Grand Army marches into Vilnius.

1831 As the result of an uprising Vilnius University is closed. Lithuania is subjected to Russification, becoming known as the 'Northwest Region'.

1915 German Army seizes Vilnius.

1918 Lithuanian council declares its country's independence.

1920–39 Poland occupies parts of southern Lithuania, including Vilnius.

1939 Hitler and Stalin sign the secret Molotov–Ribbentrop Pact.

1941 Germans occupy Vilnius.

1944 Soviet Army occupies Vilnius.

1989 A 2-million-person chain links Vilnius with Tallinn in protest against 50 years of the Molotov–Ribbentrop Pact.

1990 The Supreme Council of Lithuania demands the withdrawal of Soviet forces and an independent Lithuanian state.

1991 Soviets storm parliamentary building and TV Tower; 14 are killed.

1993 Vilnius Old Town becomes a UNESCO World Heritage Site.

2004 Lithuania joins NATO and EU. President Rolandas Paksas is impeached for involvement in a campaign funds scandal. President Valdas Adamkus is elected in his place.

WHERE TO GO

Most of the essential sights of Vilnius are conveniently located in a relatively compact area on the south bank of the Neris River. The centre of attention, justifiably, is the Old Town, a beautifully preserved, largely baroque gem, which covers 3.6 sq km (1½ sq mile) and is protected as a UNESCO World Heritage listed site. This guide subdivides the Old Town into areas defined by main attractions or districts – Vilnius Cathedral and Gediminas Castle, the Gates of Dawn (Aušros Vartai), and the central part of the Old Town between the Town Hall and the University.

Pylimo Street, with its reminders of Jewish Vilnius, marks one edge of the Old Town. To the west is the 19th-century New Town, or city centre, where sights on and around Gedimino Avenue recall the city's Soviet past. To the east is the bohemian district of Užupis.

More distant parts of Vilnius, which require public transport to reach, include Rasų cemetery, the Television Tower, Vingis Park and the Antakalnis district. The guide also includes a number of day trips for those with the time to go beyond Vilnius. A trip to historic Trakai is particularly recommended.

Note that buildings in the city are constantly under reconstruction or renovation, particularly in the warmer

The Old Town viewed from the Hill of Three Crosses

An elevated vista of the Old Town's charming mixture of architectural styles can be had from several spots, including Kalnų parkas, Crooked Hill and Gediminas Hill. However, the view of the Old Town from the Tores restaurant (*see page 140*) in Užupis is very hard to beat. Head for the restaurant's terrace in summer.

months, and public areas can close with little or no warning. Travellers need to be bold, knock on closed doors, turn on the charm and say, *'Galima?'* ('May I?'), as Vilnius isn't always aware that it's now a major tourist centre. The worst an intrepid traveller might face is an enthusiastic amateur historian, eager to explain significant historical events at length no matter how little they are understood.

AROUND THE CATHEDRAL AND CASTLE

Cathedral Square (Katedros aikštė) sits at the intersection of the two main parts of Vilnius: the city centre's main street, Gedimino Avenue, and the Old Town. The cathedral dwarfs most structures in the vicinity, making it one of the most prominent features of the city, and six new bells installed in 2002 in the separate 52m (170ft) bell tower make doubly sure you don't miss it. During the 14th century the lowest portion of the tower actually served as part of the city's fortifications; the second and third tiers were added in the 16th century, when it began to be used as a bell tower. In the 17th century the top portion and the clock were installed to give a more neoclassical look to echo the cathedral's aesthetic. In the evenings the bell tower and cathedral are lit up to great effect, making the square a good place for a post-dinner stroll. On the eastern side of the square is a monument to the city's founder, Grand Duke Gediminas, erected in 1996. The statue's creator, Vytautas Kašuba, a Lithuanian émigré to the United States, decided to place Gediminas alongside his horse (instead of astride it) to show his preference for diplomacy over war.

When walking from the cathedral entrance to the bell tower keep an eye out for a small tile marked *stebuklas*, which means miracle. Some believe that the tile is historically significant as it marks the place where a chain of nearly two million people stretching from Vilnius to Tallinn began. Although a romantic idea, this is unfortunately untrue. However, there is a belief that

Facade of Vilnius Cathedral, with bell tower beside

when one stands on the tile, makes a wish and turns around in a complete circle, the wish will be granted as long as it is kept secret. Superstitious types should keep in mind that it is considered bad luck to explain the exact location of the tile.

Vilnius Cathedral

Vilnius Cathedral (or, to give its full title, Sts Stanislaus and Vladislaus Cathedral) is the most important structure historically and culturally in the city. The area has always been the focal point of Vilnius. In pagan times, an altar or temple stood here. A cathedral was built on the site by King Mindaugas' decree in the 13th century, but it reverted to being a pagan shrine after his death. The current building dates from 1419, but the mixture of baroque, neoclassical and Renaissance styles is the result of numerous periods of rebuilding and renovation following fire and storm damage. The cathedral took on its present-day, mostly neoclassical styling in the late 18th century by the architect Laurynas Stuoka-Gucevičius and later by the Latvian architect Michael Schultz. One of the exterior's few remaining baroque features is the dome over St Casimir's chapel on the southeast corner. Most of the cathedral was completed by the end of the 19th century. Closed by the Soviets in 1950, the Cathedral became an art gallery, but was reinstated as a place of worship in 1989.

The three figures standing on top of the entrance are St Stanislaus, the patron saint of Poland, St Helena, mother of the Roman Emperor Constantine, who according to tradition found the True Cross in AD326, and St Casimir, the patron saint of Lithuania. The original figures, made by Stuoka-Gucevičius, were removed by the Soviet authorities; what you see today are replicas, placed here in 1997. The six Tuscan

The Chapel of St Casimir and the Crypt

Within the chapel of St Casimir there are numerous silver ornaments in the shape of legs, arms and other body parts. These ex-votos represent ailments and are placed by pilgrims near the tomb of St Casimir, which is believed to have healing powers. More of them can also be found along the sides of the chapel inside the Gates of Dawn *(see page 35)*.

The cathedral crypt, downstairs from behind the altar, is the final resting place for many of Lithuania's noblemen and archbishops. The floors are believed to have been relaid at least a dozen times over the centuries and many more bodies are thought to be interred below the floor, including Grand Duke Vytautas. In 1931 several coffins were discovered under the cathedral. Two belonged to the wives of Grand Duke Sigismund Augustus. The remains were transferred to the Sovereigns' Mausoleum, directly under St Casimir's chapel. The crypt also has a fresco of the crucifixion, which remained concealed until 1985. Analysis shows that it was painted around the end of the 14th century, making it the oldest wall painting in the country.

columns supporting the neo-classical portico are made less severe and more lively by the recessed statues behind them of the evangelists: Matthew with an angel, Mark with a lion, Luke with a bull and John with an eagle. Abraham and Moses are on either side of them. The tympanum – the triangular space over the door – is Tomassa Righi's *Noah's Offering,* which depicts animals on their way to being sacrificed. The Italian also sculpted all the structures on the facade.

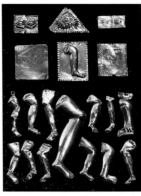

Votive offerings in the Chapel of St Casimir

Inside, the facade is mimicked by the four Doric columns and portico above the main altar. Although the church maintains clean neoclassical lines there are numerous little flourishes throughout – note that the vaulted ceilings are held up by pillars topped by rosettes and oak leaves. On the columns of the central nave hang large paintings of the 12 apostles by Pranciškus Smuglevičius, who also painted *The Martyrdom of St Stanislaus* behind the high altar. The neoclassical portico behind the altar, built by Schultz, is a rich medley of gold and silver punctuated by green marble columns.

Two of the highlights of the cathedral are the crypt and, to the left of the altar, the **Chapel of St Casimir** *(see opposite).* This is the largest and most prominent of the cathedral's 10 chapels. Its baroque styling, with black and brown marble accented by sandstone, was left untouched by Stuoka-Gucevičiu's renovations.

Chapel of St Casimir

St Casimir was the second son of Casimir Jogaillon and a member of the Jogaila dynasty, hence the eight wooden 17th-century statues of Lithuanian rulers from the Gediminas and Jogaila dynasties inside the chapel. Born in 1485, St Casimir was sent to Hungary at the age of 13 to assume the throne to which his mother believed she had a claim. He was unsuccessful and on his return his father imprisoned him for his failure. Most historians cite this as the turning point in his life. Young Casimir became an aesthete, praying constantly and giving up all earthly pleasures. After his release he found favour with his father and became the heir-apparent. However, his health deteriorated and he died at the age of 25 from tuberculosis. He was buried in the sanctuary of the cathedral (unlike most noblemen who were buried in the cathedral's crypt), which later became this chapel. This burial choice was a result of the regard in which the young man was held in Poland and Lithuania, heightened by the fact that soon after his death numerous miracles were attributed to him.

Completed in 1636, the chapel is also one of the oldest intact parts of the building. The two frescoes along the sides of the chapel are by Michaelangelo Palloni; both depict the miracle of St Casimir's coffin, which allegedly when opened in 1614, 130 years after his death, revealed a barely decomposed body giving off a fragrant odour. The 18th-century coffin on the altar holds the remains of the saint and is believed to have miracle-working powers. The 16th-century portrait of *Three-handed St Casimir* with a silver overlay, also located in the chapel, is the result of a miracle, according to legend. The artist is supposed to have tried to paint over a hand that he had decided had been painted in the wrong position. He painted another hand in another place, but the extra hand kept re-appearing; eventually the artist decided to retain the third appendage.

The Castle

Although some visitors may enjoy walking up to the top of the 50m (165ft) high **Gediminas Hill**, most people opt to take the funicular to reach **Gediminas Tower** and the **Upper Castle Museum** (Aukštutinės pilies muziejus; open May–Sept: daily 10am–7pm; Oct–Apr: daily 10am–5pm; admission fee). The tower is the restored western keep of the castle. Made of brick and dating from the 14th century, it is considered to be one of the symbols of Vilnius; there used to be three towers, surrounded by a defensive wall, but this is all that's left.

Gediminas Tower

The 80 steps inside the keep wind around the thick-walled structure to the top, where there's a wonderful view. From the top of the building you can see most of the Old Town and the central parts of the city. Inside the tower are small exhibition spaces for models

Lithuanian National Museum

of the castle complex through the ages and displays of armoury and weapons from the 14th to 18th centuries.

It's a pleasant stroll downhill to the archaeological site of the **Lower Castle** (Žemutinės Pilies Muziejus; tel: 261 40 63). From the 16th century, this grand building was the Royal Palace and residence of Lithuania's grand dukes and their families. Tsarist officials demolished it in the late 18th century. The Lithuanian government plans to rebuild the structure by 2009.

Lithuanian National Museum

Below the castle, on the banks of the Neris River, stands the **Lithuanian National Museum** (Lietuvos nacionalinis muziejus; open Wed–Sat 10am–6pm; Sun 10am–3pm; admission fee). Located in the New Arsenal building, the museum is dedicated to the history of the country, with an emphasis on folk culture. Farming, fishing and woodworking equipment are displayed alongside national costumes and folk art, and there are recreations of the interiors of traditional rural wooden houses. Another section of the museum deals with weapons, armour and paintings from the 14th century up until World War II. The statue of the only king of Lithuania, Mindaugas, in front of the museum, was unveiled on the 750th anniversary of his coronation on 6 July 2003.

Just past the National Museum, on Arsenalo Street, is the **Museum of Applied Arts** (Taikomosios dailės muziejus; open Tues–Sat 11am–6pm; Sun 11am–4pm; admission fee). The main exhibition changes every few months, but it usually focuses on Lithuanian works of art with a religious dimension. For the most part the small permanent collection is of monstrances and other Christian art made in gold, silver and precious jewels, with a few paintings and folk pieces sprinkled throughout.

Crooked Hill

At the foot of the castle is wooded **Kalnų Park**, a good place in the warmer months for a pleasant break after exploring the castle area. On hot days, vendors selling anything cold from ice cream to beer, station themselves throughout the area. From the park, cross the tiny Vilnia River and head onto the **Crooked Hill** (Kreivasis kalnas). Adjacent to Gediminas Hill, this is where, according to legend, 14 Franciscan monks were martyred by the still very pagan Lithuanians some time during the 14th century. Seven were allegedly hacked to pieces and another seven were tied to wooden crosses and sent down the Neris back west from whence they came. The three white crosses that stand here today are reproductions of early 20th-century ones (which had replaced earlier ones) that were taken down during Stalinist times. One of the best views of the Old Town is your reward for climbing the hill.

AROUND THE GATES OF DAWN

At the southern end of the Old Town lies the 16th-century
Gates of Dawn (Aušros Vartai), a magnet for tourists and
pilgrims alike. This is the sole surviving gate of the city's
nine-gate fortifications, and its original defensive purpose
can be seen in the round holes at the top of the structure,
through which cannon were aimed. On the top portion
of the southern side of the monument is the Lithuanian
state emblem, Vytis, a white knight on a steed against a
red background.

The road leading out of this area led to the town of Medininkai, and the gate was originally called the Medininkai
gate. Carmelite nuns re-named it in 1671 when they built a

The Duke and the Duchess

The second wife of the Grand Duke Sigismund Augustus (1548–72)
was the renowned widowed beauty Barbora Radvilaitė. Some specu-
late that an affair had preceded the nuptials and archaeological digs
have revealed a small underground corridor that would have connected their two residences. Although they married, her acceptance into
the Polish-based monarchy was slow because her wealthy family was
openly nationalistic about being Lithuanian. In 1548, Barbora was
titled the Grand Duchess of Lithuania. The couple moved to Kraków
after the death of Sigismund's father in order for him to assume
the throne of the Polish–Lithuanian Commonwealth. In May 1551 a
mysterious long-running illness took the duchess' life in Kraków. At the
time of her death many believed her mother-in-law, Bona Sforza, had
poisoned her. One of Barbora's last requests was to be buried in Vilnius,
and today her sarcophagus can be found in the crypt of Vilnius Cathedral. Local legend dictates that the face of the Virgin Mary in the Gates
of Dawn is a portrait of the legendary beauty.

(handwritten: from the old town door on the left go up the stairs)

chapel inside it to house a sacred image of the Virgin Mary (a chapel of some sort was usually located in a city gate to offer protection and a provide a place for last-minute prayers before a trip). To reach the interior of the chapel, face the Old Town, walk under the gate and enter an unmarked building on the right. A stone stair-case leads into the chapel, which is dominated by its reputedly miracle-working icon, which is also visible from the street. **The Blessed**

The chapel of the Madonna built within the Gates of Dawn

Virgin Mary: Mother of Mercy, a large painting overlaid in silver and gold, was painted some time in the 17th century over an earlier icon on the same eight oak panels. The painting's powers, recognised by the Pope in 1773, have made the chapel into one of the most renowned pilgrimage sites in the country, and you will see kneeling pilgrims praying to the icon. The present-day neoclassical style of the chapel is the result of a renovation of its earlier baroque features in 1829.

Church of St Teresa

The adjacent **Church of St Teresa** (Šv Teresės Bažnyčia) was the home of the Carmelite nuns who built the Gates of Dawn chapel. The convent grounds and building have been divided into private property, but the church is still used. Dating from the early 17th century, it is one of the oldest baroque churches in the city, and its facade is possibly more striking than its interior. Huge scrolls along either side of the top tier are particularly eye-catching. Of note in the interior is the metal rococo pulpit and the painting of *The Apotheosis of St Teresa* above the rococo altar.

Church of the Holy Spirit

Aušros Vartų, the street leading north from the Gates of Dawn, is one of the most pounded pieces of pavement in the city. Between the baroque churches are numerous shops and cafés catering to locals as well as tourists. At No. 7 the **art gallery Arka** (open Tues–Fri noon–7pm, Sat noon–4pm) has an impressive collection of local and international art, much of which integrates amber and religion – two

Church of the Holy Spirit

things that seem to be the theme of the street. At No. 17 is **Jonas Bugailiškis Art Studio**. The man himself can often be seen at work, shaping a piece of wood. Most of the work in this workshop-gallery is based on Lithuanian folk art carvings, but the pieces all transcend anything sold on the streets. The opening hours depend on the whim of the artist.

Depending on how open the church gate is, the tree-lined courtyard of the 17th-century Orthodox **Church of the Holy Spirit** (Stačiatikių Šventosios Dvasios cerkvė) can be seen at No. 10 Aušros Vartų. Inside the church, your eye is drawn to the bright green iconostasis, a large screen dividing the altar from the rest of the church, which was built by Jan Krzyzstof Glaubitz in the 1750s. In front of the iconostasis and covered by a baldachin are the miraculously preserved **bodies of three martyrs** (Saints Anthony, Eustachius and Ivan), dressed in red robes (white at Christmas, black during Lent). The trio, who served at the court of the pagan Grand Duke Algirdas, were martyred for their faith in 1347; they were canonised in 1373. Orthodox Christians believe that the bodies have healing powers, which are exceptionally strong on 26 June when they are left naked.

Basilian Gate

The **Basilian Gate** (Bazilijonų vartai) is another captivating piece of architecture on Aušros Vartų. Built in 1761 by Jan Krzyzstof Glaubitz in the late baroque style, the arch is exceptionally ornate, with curved lines on its cornices, scrolls and open pediments. The bas-relief at the top depicts the Holy Trinity, and below is the all-seeing eye of God.

The gate forms the entrance to the Gothic **Basilian monastery**, including the **Church of the Holy Trinity** (Šv Trejybės cerkvė). The site has a complex history. In 1347, Juliana, wife of Grand Duke Algirdas, had a wooden church built here, which in 1514 was replaced by a stone Orthodox Church. From 1608 to 1827 the church and the monastery belonged to the Uniate (Greek-Catholic) Basilian monks, before returning to the Orthodox Church. The Soviets used it as a workshop and after Lithuania's independence it was returned to the Basilian Uniates. Restoration work has unearthed frescoes thought to date from the 16th century. The **bell tower** is the only structure left untouched by the changes of ownership and styles and is close to its original 16th-century design.

Restored houses on Town Hall Square

The monastery also underwent numerous changes. Most notably the south portion was used as a prison in the first part of the 19th century. The poet **Adam Mick-iewicz** (1798–1855), along with other members of the perceived anti-tsarist movements in Vilnius University, was imprisoned between 1823–4, an event commemorated in a plaque above one of the doors. In 1920 an architecture scholar, Juliusz Klos, determined which cell had been used by Mickiewicz and a Latin plaque was put up. In English it reads: 'Gustav died here on 1 November 1823; Conrad was born here on 1 November 1823.'
This is a reference to Mickiewicz's *The Forefather's Eve*, where an imprisoned man named Gustav has an epiphany, deciding to change his perspective from the personal to that of his nation, and marking the change by altering his name to Conrad.

Further along Aušros Vartų, just before Town Hall Square, you will reach the **Church of St Casimir** (Šv Kazimiero Bažnyčia), dedicated to the patron saint of Lithuania. Founded by the Jesuits in 1604, the church was built to resemble the order's mother church, Il Gesù, in Rome. The large dome was added during reconstruction in the 1750s. In a supremely chequered history the church has been used

for grain storage by Napoleon's troops, turned into an Orthodox church in tsarist times, made a Lutheran Protestant church by the Germans during World War I, and served as a Museum of Atheism in the Soviet era. It was returned to the Catholic Church in 1987.

TOWN HALL TO UNIVERSITY

Just past the church, Aušros Vartų gives way to Didžioji at the Town Hall Square. Dominating the square is the stately neoclassical former **Town Hall** (Rotušė; open Mon–Fri 10am–6pm, Sat 10am–4pm; closed Sun; admission fee). The building was completed in 1799 by the architect Laurynas

Stuoka-Gucevičius, who also worked on Vilnius Cathedral. The main point of interest is the **Great Hall** (Didžioji Salė) – used for concerts in the early 19th century – which houses some exhibits on the history of the site and a number of small art galleries which comprise the **Artists' Palace**.

Artillery Bastion

To the east of the Town Hall is the **Artillery Bastion** (Artilerijos bastėja; Bokšto 20; open Tues–Sat 10am–5pm, Sun 10am–3pm; admission fee), which makes a nice change of pace from the baroque, religious world nearby. Built in the 17th century to reinforce the town's fortifications, the red-brick, semi-circular structure fell into disuse and decay during the 18th century. It came to be used first as an orphanage, then a rubbish site, then a vegetable store. Nowadays it houses a small museum of old weapons and armour. The main

Inside the Artillery Bastion

attraction is the good view of the Old Town from the top of the bastion.

Return to the Town Hall, and turn north down Didžioji Street. Those interested in seeing a cross section of Lithuanian paintings, drawings and sculpture from the 16th to 19th centuries might

> **Legend has it that inside the Artillery Bastion lived a dragon, the Vilnius Basilisk, which would on occasion leave his lair and turn people to stone with his gaze – until he saw his own reflection in a mirror.**

like to visit the **Vilnius Picture Gallery** (Vilniaus paveikslų galerija; open Tues–Sat noon–6pm, Sun noon–5pm; closed Mon; admission fee). The building is a converted palace that once belonged to the Chodkevičių (in Polish, Chodkiewicz) family.

Not far away, along the same street, is the Orthodox **Church of St Paraskeva** (Pyatnickaya cerkvė), built on a pagan site dedicated to Ragutis, god of beer. To the left of the entrance are two trees, between which is a large stone with a hole for a fire, believed to have been part of the original pagan structure. The building came into being as a Christian church in 1345. The last renovations, in 1865, were by Nicholai Tchiagin. A plaque in Russian to the left of the church entrance tells the apocryphal story of how Ibrahim Hannibal, an Ethiopian prince and 'grandfather' (actually great-grandfather) of the writer Alexander Pushkin (1799–1837) was baptised here in 1705 when Tsar Peter the Great, his patron, was visiting the church.

Dominikonų Street

Straddling one side of Vilnius University, **Dominikonų Street**, is a good example of the picturesque byways of the Old Town. This curved street has many intact historic buildings, which accommodate a number of antiques shops. The street takes its name from the imposing **Dominican Church of the Holy Spirit** (Šventosios Dvasios bažnyčia), one of the major focal points of the Polish-speaking Catholic community in Vilnius. Don't be put off by the beggars in the archway or the long, dimly lit hallway leading into the church, as the interior is nothing short of breathtaking, with a number of arresting fixtures, paintings and frescoes. One of the most captivating, with its rings of clouds sailing up through the heavens, is the fresco of the **Apotheosis of the Holy Spirit** around the cupola. To the right of the centre aisle is the 20th-century **Mercy of God painting of Christ**, depicting a vision by Sister Faustyna Kowalska (1905–38), who was beatified in 1993. The painting is believed by the faithful to have miracle-working powers. In the 33m (108ft) long **crypt**, closed to the public, are the mummified corpses of nearly 2,000 victims of the Napoleonic wars.

Along the street outside are a couple of architectural features to look for. Above the restaurant at No. 9 notice the four lion faces below the second-storey window and the deer over the top of the building. The neoclassical style was

A Supernatural Happening

According to legend, a Russian guard was placed inside the Church of the Holy Spirit after Russian authorities were notified of strange sounds in the area at night. Towards the end of his first night's shift he heard pounding, thumping and cries of anguish, which escalated in volume until finally he saw the figure of a cloaked woman emerge from a brick wall. Terrified, he ran to find help. When he returned with a detachment of soldiers, the church was silent, so they quickly set about tearing down the wall from which the apparition had appeared. The crypt's existence was then revealed.

added to No. 11 after a fire in 1748 by its owner, Alexander Pociejus, a governor of Trakai, although elements of its early baroque origins can be seen in the two bas-reliefs of St George and St Michael.

Tucked in a side street off Dominikonų there is a small gallery/workspace where a group of artists have their **Young Artists' Old Town Studio** (Totorių 22). Although quite small and open only when one or more of the artists needs the space for working, it is a gem in the contemporary Lithuanian art scene.

Dominican Church of the Holy Spirit

Vilnius University

Taking up more than a block of the Old Town around 13 linked courtyards is **Vilnius University** (Vilniaus universitetas; courtyards open Mon–Sat 10am–5pm; admission fee). Founded in 1579 by Jesuits, and run by them for more than 200 years, the university became one of the most esteemed centres of learning in Polish-speaking Europe. It was closed between 1832 and 1921, because the Russian government believed it to be a hot-bed of anti-tsarist sentiment – which it was.

The university is bordered by Pilies, Skapo and Šv Jono streets and has gates leading onto each of these, but only the Universiteto entrance is consistently open. Directly across from the exit sits the **Presidential Palace**, whose clean neoclassical lines loom over Daukanto square.

The main entrance has a map of the university's layout and a small window where you pay an admission fee that covers the entrance to the grounds and allows you to take pictures inside the 13 stunning courtyards. It's worth keeping in mind that, when the window is unmanned, individual visitors or those in small groups can in most cases enter without paying.

The first courtyard is named in honour of the poet and humanist M. Sarbievijus (1595–1640). Directly across from the entrance stands a 19th-century building which houses Littera, the university bookshop, marked on its interior by frescoes painted in the late 1970s. An interesting **fresco** on the interior of the building can be reached up the flight of stairs next door to the bookshop. The entire hall is

Presidential Palace

given over to scenes from the life of Lithuanian peasantry, with an emphasis on their Baltic traditions.

To the right of the bookshop, through the passageway and up the stairs, is a broad, open piazza and the impressive ring of arched galleries of the **Grand** or **Skarga Courtyard**. On the south side is the Aula or assembly hall, designed by Michael Shultz, who also worked on Vilnius Cathedral. The figures in the recessed cavity personify Truth and

Sarbievijus Courtyard at Vilnius University

Beauty. The Italian architects commissioned by king of the Commonwealth, Stephen Bathory, in the 1570s brought an open design to the building, which was not entirely suited to Lithuania's climate. (Some of the original galleries in the university's main building later had to be bricked in.)

The squat, heavy arches of the galleries are in contrast to the more whimsical and baroque facade of **St Johns' Church** (Švs Jonų bažnyčia), which stands at the edge of the yard. The church, named after both St John the Baptist and St John the Evangelist, was built in 1427, but its present baroque texture is the work of Jan Krzyzstof Glaubitz, who is responsible for numerous other works in the city, including the Basilian Gate *(see page 37)*. The adjacent 68m (223ft) bell tower is the tallest structure in the Old Town. Sts Johns' is both a museum and a parish church – some of the items displayed are leftovers from the Soviet era when the church housed a Museum of Scientific Thought.

➤   Opposite the church, another passageway leads to the 16th-century **Observatory Courtyard**. The Astronomical Observatory here was founded in 1753 and designed by Professor of Astronomy and Mathematics, Tomas Žebrauskas. The building is decorated by astrological or zodiac symbols and below the frieze is a quote from Virgil, which translates as: 'Courage illuminated the old world with light.' The plaque further down the building reads: 'This house belongs to Uranus: down with petty troubles, the contemptible earth is disdained here, from here the way leads to the stars.' Inside the building, the White Hall should not be missed for its **two sculptures of the Greek deities**, Uranus, god of the sky, and Diana, goddess of the moon. Diana is also goddess of the hunt, an ironic, if unintentional allusion to the search for academic funding: she is holding a portrait of Elžbieta Oginskytė-Puzinienė, the main benefactor of the original building.

To the left of the entrance is a small courtyard dominated by a tree. Further along is the Daukanto courtyard, which surrounds part of the Philology Department. In one corner is the office of the **Yiddish Studies Centre**. The first of its kind in post-Holocaust Eastern Europe, it holds popular Yiddish-language summer courses. Through the double doors and down the hallway, the Department of Philology library is worth visiting for its fresco of the **Four Seasons**.

Pilies Street

Bordering the university on its eastern edge, **Pilies Street** offers a welcome diversion in the form of local artists selling their wares and musicians playing guitar or accordion. The street is also home to the **Vilnius Art Academy Gallery** (Pilies 44/2; open Mon–Sat noon–6pm), which has a small collection of photographs and some interesting graphic art.

Head down Pilies and turn right into Bernardinų Street, one of the Old Town's most atmospheric lanes, with its rows of

Zodiac signs in the Observatory Courtyard

17th- and 18th-century mansions. The **Adam Mickiewicz Memorial Room Museum** (Mickevičiaus memorialinis butas-muziejis; Bernardinų 11; open Tues–Fri 10am–5pm, Sat–Sun 10am–2pm) is just what the lengthy name would lead one to believe it is. The Polish-language poet lived here in 1822 and is reported to have finished his poem *Grazyna* while staying here with a professor. Three rooms inside are filled with translations of the poet's work into other languages and a few pieces of furniture he is thought to have used.

PYLIMO STREET

Pylimo Street marks the western edge of the Old Town. In this area it is **Vokiečių gatvė** (German Street) that dominates, especially in summer when this tree-lined thoroughfare, which is split by parkland, is alive with outdoor cafés. The first known mention of the street is from 1576, making it one of the oldest in the city. The name is a reminder of a time when large

On the outside of Rūdninkų 18, just off Pylimo Street, there is a map showing the outlines of the two largest wartime Jewish ghettos in Vilnius, where the city's Jewish population was interred before their deportation to the death camps.

numbers of foreign (probably German) traders lived there. The area to the north and south of it later became the Jewish ghetto. The buildings on the western side date for the most part from before World War II, but almost every building on the eastern side had to be rebuilt after the area was heavily bombed.

At the southern end of Vokiečių is the **Contemporary Arts Centre** (Šiuolaikinio meno centras; open Tues–Sun 11am–7pm; closed Mon; admission fee), which generally holds temporary exhibitions, although there is one permanent display, the **Fluxus room**, containing numerous works by the 1960s Fluxus Movement. Perhaps the best known member of this group was John Lennon's paramour, **Yoko Ono**, and some of her wallpaper designs are on display. There is also an information lab, which is open to the public.

Radvilos Palace

Along Vilniaus Street stands the palace of the Radvilos family (Polish, Radziwiłł), all that remains of the city estate of a noble Lithuanian family. Part of it functions as the **Radvilos Palace Museum** (Radvilų rūmai; open Tues–Sat noon–6pm, Sun noon–5pm; closed Mon; admission fee), in which close to 200 of their **family portraits** are on display, along with a small collection of foreign fine art.

Further along the street is the **Theatre, Music and Film Museum** (Lietuvos teatro, muzikos ir kino muziejus; open Tues–Fri noon–6pm, Sat 11am–4pm; closed Sun–Mon; admission fee). Most of the emphasis here is on theatre and music. There are lovely **music boxes** from the early 1800s,

pianolas and **harmoniums**, and a few theatrical costumes and set designs, most from before World War II. The cinema section is abysmal and takes up only one room.

Inside the Teacher's House (Mokytojų namai; Vilniaus 39) is what is considered the finest art gallery in the city, **Vartai** (open Tues–Fri noon–6pm, Sat noon–4pm; closed Sun–Mon). Founded in 1991, it never seems to have an empty section of wall space. Although most of the artists are Lithuanian, there are a few international ones sprinkled throughout. Expect thought-provoking pieces that centre around the schools of **naive and surrealist art**.

The Synagogue

In September 1939, Vilnius had about 100 synagogues to serve the spiritual needs of a Jewish population of approximately 57,000. The **synagogue** (open Mon–Fri, Sun

A trolleybus makes its way past the synagogue on Pylimo Street

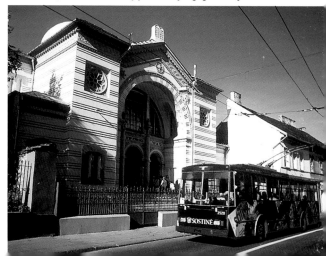

4.30–5.30pm) on Pylimo is the only one in the city to sur-
vive World War II. Built at the turn of the 20th century in a
Moorish style, it has an inscription that reads, 'A prayer
house is sacred for all nations.'

Down the street on the ground floor of Pylimo 4 is the centre for the Jewish community of Lithuania. On the second
floor is the small **Vilna Gaon Jewish State Museum of
Lithuania** (open Mon–Thur
9am–5pm, Fri 9am–4pm;
admission fee), which is
named after the Gaon of Vilnius, Elijah Ben Solomon
Zalmon (1720–97), the city's
greatest rabbinical scholar.
Photographs, drawings and a
variety of artefacts give a
sense of Jewish life before
and during the Holocaust.
An exhibition honours eth-
nic Lithuanians who risked their lives in order to save Jews
during the war. For a fuller account of the Holocaust in
Vilnius and Lithuania, visit the Museum of the Holocaust
(*see page 52*).

> The grave of the Gaon
> of Vilnius is often visited
> by those fascinated by
> the scholar. He is buried
> in the northwest out-
> skirts of town in the
> Saltoniškių cemetery
> (Saltoniškių kapinės;
> intersection of Viršu-
> liškių and Buivydiškių;
> open daily, except Sat,
> sunrise–sunset.

Tucked into Rūdninkų Street, just off Pylimo, is the
salmon-pink **Church of All Saints** (Visų Šventųjų
bažnyčia), completed in 1631. The facade is punctuated by
flat Corinthian pilasters, while the belfry, completed in
1743, provides baroque flourishes. The interior of the
church is covered with colourful **sculptures** and **frescoes**
depicting religious events.

Art and Artists

Also in the area is the **Art Niche** (Meno Niša; Basanavičiaus 1/13; open Tues–Fri noon–6pm, Sat noon–4pm), a

Sat until 4pm TUES

small shop displaying and selling jewellery and artworks by a number of local artists and craftspeople.

Continuing the artistic theme, a short walk to the west of the Old Town on Kalinausko 1 brings you to an unexpected sight: a bust of American rock musician **Frank Zappa** (1940–93). No, he wasn't Lithuanian. The memorial, erected in 1995, is simply the result of the enthusiasm of the local Zappa Fan Club, and perhaps a desire to find a replacement for the numerous Communist-era statues that were removed from the city's streets in the early 1990s.

Frank Zappa immortalised

The bust itself was cast by Konstantinas Bogdanas who, during Soviet times, had made a name for himself for his castings of Lenin's image.

CITY CENTRE

Gedimino prospektas (Gedimino Avenue), the main street of Vilnius, runs the length of the city centre – some 2km (1.2 miles), starting from the cathedral and ending at the Žvėrynas Bridge (Žvėryno tiltas), which crosses the River Neris. It was first laid out in the 1850s, and has been christened and rechristened several times since, each new name (including Mickiewicz, Hitler and Lenin) reflecting the ideology of the current ruling power.

At Gedimino 4 is the **National Drama Theatre**. The gold-faced black-clad muses guarding the entrance to the building represent Drama, Tragedy and Comedy. Further down, the statue at Gedimino 27 commemorates poet and writer **Julija Beniuševičiūtė-Žymantienė** (1845–1921). Born into a Polish aristocratic family, a defiant Julija learned to speak Lithuanian by spending time with the local serfs. Most of her work stresses the hardships of peasant life.

Three muses at the National Drama Theatre on Gedimino

Holocaust Museum

An estimated 94 percent of Lithuanian Jews were killed during the Holocaust. This devastation is explored in the small **Museum of the Holocaust**, also called the Green House (Žaliasis namas; Pamėnkalnio 12; open Mon–Thur 9am–5pm, Fri 9am–4pm; closed Sat–Sun; admission fee), in a street running parallel to Gedimino. Written accounts of mass executions and photographs of life inside the **Vilnius and Kaunas ghettoes** make for a thought-provoking and disturbing visit. Outside the museum stands a monument to **Chiune Sugihara** (1900–86), acting Japanese consul in Kaunas, Lithuania's second city, between 1939–40. Along with his colleagues, he helped save some 6,000 Jews by issuing them papers so that they could leave the country, despite the disapproval of his superiors. He continued issuing documents right up until the time his train left for Germany, and it's said that he even handed his consular stamp to a man on the platform to continue his work. Sugihara's actions came to wide public attention just before his death in 1986 as a result of pressure by many of the people he had helped to save.

Lukiškių Square

Towards the centre of Gedimino sits **Lukiškių Square** (Lukiškių aikštė), which holds a significant place in the city's history. It was here that in 1863 General Muryavov, known as the Hangman, set about executing the insurgents of that year's uprising. A small **plaque** near the church commemorates the event. Later, the square held the city's most prominent statue of Lenin. Images of its dismantling during the country's fight for independence are etched in the nation's memory. At one end of the square is the baroque **Church of St Philip and St James** (Šv Jokūbo ir Pilypo bažnyčia). On the church's northern side is a **chapel dedicated to St Hyacinth** where numerous frescoes depict the life of this saint.

On the other side of the square is the former KGB headquarters and prison, which houses the **Museum of Genocide** ◀
Victims (Genocido Aukų muziejus; open Tues–Sat 10am–5pm, Sun 10am– 3pm; admission fee). Lithuanians suspected of anti-Soviet activities were brought here, interrogated, tortured and, in many cases, executed. The names of those who perished inside are carved on the building's facade. Also outside is a **collection of stones** from all over Lithuania

Former KGB headquarters

which symbolises the far-reaching damage of the Soviet system. Tours given by former inmates in Lithuanian or Russian explain how prisoners were treated, showing the visiting cells, torture rooms and the execution chamber. Pre-recorded English audio tours are available. Be warned that the experience is very disturbing and graphic, and is not recommended for children.

Gedimino comes to an end at **Independence Square** (Nepriklausomybės aikštė), where the restoration of Lithuanian independence was declared on 11 March 1990. Ironically, the square is dominated by two Soviet-era buildings, the Seimas or **Parliamentary Palace** and the **National Library**. Named after Martynas Mažvydas, the author of the first Lithuanian book, the library sometimes hosts small exhibitions on various national and international writers, composers and musicians.

The Green Bridge, or Žaliasis tiltas

Žvėrynas District

Just across the Žvėrynas Bridge (Žvėryno tiltas) is the **Žvėrynas district**. This residential area started off as a hunting ground, and it still maintains a somewhat rural feel. Its wooden houses, complete with impressive gardens, are becoming rarer in other parts of the city as redevelopment gains pace.

Žvėrynas has two striking sights. Silver-coloured Byzantine-style cupolas mark the Russian Orthodox **Znamenskaya Church** or Church of the Apparition of the Theotokos (Dievo Motinos Ženklo iš Dangaus cerkvė). The building dates from 1903.

To the left of the church on a parallel street is the Moorish-looking Karaite house of worship or **Kenesa**, which was built in the 1920s. Members of the Karaite community, who practise an Old Testament-based religion that has some similarities with Judaism, were brought to Vilnius from their homeland near the Black Sea by Grand Duke Vytautus in the 14th century. The Soviet-era government closed the Kenesa and used it as a warehouse, but the building is once again a house of worship.

The Green Bridge

On the northern side of Gedimino, the Green Bridge (Žaliasis tiltas) heads over the Neris into the Šnipiškės district. The structure, built in 1952, is unremarkable except for the 3–4m (10–13ft) high statues that adorn each of its corners. These Socialist Realist pieces depict sturdy-looking figures in various poses, representing agriculture, industry, peace and youth. Most statues from Soviet times have been taken down and moved to Grūtas Park *(see page 68)*, but these ones have been allowed to stay as reminders of how art in the Soviet era was manipulated to serve the state's totalitarian ends.

EAST OF THE OLD TOWN

St Anne's Church

Back in the Old Town, on Maironio Street, is a gem of a building and one of the symbols of Vilnius. **St Anne's Church** (Šv Onos bažnyčia) was constructed in the 16th century in Gothic style. Its builders used 33 types of decorative brick to create its facade of pointed-arch windows, delicate towers and elegant spires. According to tradition, Napoleon was so enamoured of the structure that he wished to take it back to France with him in the palm of his hand. The exterior may be a masterpiece, but the interior is rather bland.

> **Just to the side of St Anne's is a 1984 statue commemorating Adam Mickiewicz, the pre-eminent 19th-century Polish poet and nationalist. The split column upon which he leans is meant to symbolise Mickiewicz's divided feelings about his Polish roots on the one hand, and his adopted city of Vilnius on the other.**

Tucked away behind St Anne's is the much larger and more restrained-looking **Bernadine Church** (Bernadinų bažnyčia). The church was built in 1525 in Gothic style, but the facade was later given a Renaissance makeover, and most of the interior is in the baroque style. During the Polish-Lithuanian uprising of 1863, the Russians saw the church as a den of anti-tsarist agitation and turned it into army barracks. Later, during the Soviet occupation, the church was the headquarters of the Vilnius Art Academy. The interior frescoes, which date from the 16th century, are slowly being restored.

Further along the Vilnia River is the Orthodox **Church of the Dormition of the Holy Mother of God** (Skaisčiausios Dievo Motinos cerkvė). Although built in the 14th century by Grand Duke Algirdas for his Orthodox wife, the vagaries of history led to it being used successively as an archive, army barracks, warehouse, smithy and anatomy lab. Most of the building you see today is the result of work carried out in the 1860s. The most interesting part of the church is the interior, with its five-tiered, extremely detailed **iconostasis**.

The **Church of St Michael** (Šv Mykolo bažnyčia) lies in the Old Town, but is just a few steps from Užupis. The mustard-coloured building has some striking items – rosette ceilings, ornate baroque altars and numerous lunettes – which are indicative of its late 16th-century construction.

Užupis

On the other side of the Vilnia River from the Old Town is the **Užupis** district. Its rundown 19th-century buildings have been colonised by the bohemian set, making it a focal point of unconventional ideas and non-mainstream art. Užupis has a ramshackle charm, and though property prices have been

Polish poet Adam Mickiewicz and St Anne's Church

Constitution wall in Užupis

rising sharply in recent years – as an increasing number of wealthy people move in – a large group of artists, musicians and general non-conformists remains to keep the rest of the city on its toes.

Every year on 1 April (April Fool's Day) the residents celebrate the Independence Day of their self-declared 'break-away republic'. A border patrol is set up around the neighbourhood with fake policemen checking and stamping passports. The Užupis Republic has an ambassador in Moscow, an army of 12, and diplomatic relations with the Lithuanian Ministry of Foreign Affairs. Its constitution can be seen on a wall at the eastern end of Paupio Street, written in both English and Lithuanian on mirrored surfaces. The statutes list the rights of the republic's citizens and, according to Article No. 12, a dog has the right to be a dog and (No. 13) a cat doesn't have to love its owner, but in times of difficulty it is required to help its owner. The only requirement of people is that they must remember their names. The last three articles are: Don't defeat, Don't defend and Don't surrender.

Many of the republic's denizens can usually be found at the very pleasant Užupis Café (Užupio kavinė; open 10am–11pm) by the river. Further down from the café is the **Alternative Arts Centre** (Alternatyvaus meno centras), which acts as the headquarters for the Užupis Ministry of Culture. The building is usually empty, but a few pieces of artwork can sometimes be found in and around the vicinity. The only work with seeming permanence is the *faux* washing machine made of stone; however, a walk down the path beside the building in summer can often surprise the visitor with some pieces of artwork left for others to appreciate. For those not willing to search for their art there is also the **Užupis Gallery** (Užupio galerija; Užupio 3; open Tues–Fri 11am–7pm, Sat 11am–5pm; closed Sun–Mon) where you can often watch someone creating the metal pieces hanging inside the gallery.

The Glass Bead Game Gallery (Stiklo karoliukai; Paupio 2/9) plays host to local and international exhibitions, as well as staging film and music evenings. The gallery is named after Herman Hesse's 1943 novel of the same name, and claims to be the only place in Lithuania where the game in question (invented by Hesse and with a series of incomprehensible 'rules') is played.

At the junction of Užupio and Malūnų Streets is a small square with the republic's only monument, a statue of an

Glassblower's wall painting

The Angel of Užupis

Angel blowing a trumpet atop a pillar. Inside a courtyard opposite is **The Black Ceramics Centre** (Juodosis keramikos centras; open Tues–Sat noon–6pm; closed Sun–Mon). This workshop and gallery space is dedicated to the art of black ceramics, which are made using a technique that originated in Persia around the 6th century. By leaving the clay unglazed, the iron in it forms a layer on the surface when fired, making the object waterproof and giving it a distinctive black metallic sheen. Also of note in the neighbourhood is the **Intro Gallery** (Maironio 3; open daily 10am–6pm), where a wide range of cutting-edge artworks can be found on display.

For a rest from sightseeing, try the **Bernardine cemetery**, at the southeastern portion of Užupis, perched above the river. Among its mostly 19th-century gravestones are the resting places of many Vilnius University professors, scientists and painters.

Another tranquil location is pine-covered Kalnų Park *(see page 33)*, which is accessible from northern Užupis.

OUTLYING AREAS

Antakalnis

The **Antakalnis** suburb makes up most of the northeast part of the city. The name means 'on a hill', although the area is surprisingly flat. In the 17th century Lithuanian nobility built mansions along the banks of the Neris here. Few have survived and the skyline now is marked by a large number of Soviet-era housing complexes. The **Church of Sts Peter and Paul** (Švs Petro ir Povilo bažnyčia; Antakalnio 1) stands apart from this dreary scene. The church was built in the latter half of the 17th century to commemorate the departure of Russian forces. Its sumptuous interior, created by two Italian craftsmen, has an astonishing number of **white stucco fixtures**, including some 2,000 pieces of statuary. The visual onslaught is overwhelming, yet the only colour comes from the ceiling frescoes depicting St Peter. As one looks up, the eye is first drawn to the large and impressive **boat-shaped chandelier**, installed in 1905. Outside is John Paul II Square (Jono Pauliaus II aikštė), named in honour of the Pope's visit in 1993.

Organ in the Church of Sts Peter and Paul

About 1km (½ mile) northwest of the church lies the **Antakalnis cemetery** (Antakalnio kapinės; Kariū Kapū 11; open daily sunrise–sunset), where the country's complicated 20th-century history is writ large. Near the entrance are rows of white, plain headstones of the Polish soldiers killed in World War I; beyond are the remnants of the **Soviet-era cemetery**, with an eternal flame that has been allowed to go out; in the centre is a large *pietà* rising from among the graves of victims of the Soviets, including Lithuanian partisans and the border guards murdered by the Soviets at Medininkai on 31 July 1991. Elsewhere, a small memorial commemorates the **soldiers of Napoleon's army** who died in Vilnius *(see page 18)*.

Rasų Cemetery

Rasų Cemetery

Southwest of the city centre is the Rasos district. The main attraction here is Rasų cemetery (Rasū kapinės; intersection of Rasū and Sukilėliū; open daily sunrise–sunset). Its large number of trees give the place a rural atmosphere and, when the leaves start to turn golden in the autumn, provide a visual spectacle rare in most cities. A number of historical figures are buried here. Chief among them is the **General Józef Piłsudski**, a Vilnius-educated Pole who became president of Poland in 1919. Although he was not beloved by Lithuanians (it was his campaign that put Vilnius and parts of southern Lithuania under Polish control from 1920 to 1939), he had a strong attachment to Vilnius and wished his heart to be buried there. The rest of his body is interred in Wawel Castle in Kraków. On 1 November, All Souls' Day, members of the Polish community of Vilnius set a small bonfire around the grave to celebrate his accomplish-

Paneriai, on the way to Trakai, is the site of the mass murder by the Nazis of some 100,000 civilians, mostly Jews. Located less than 10 km (6 miles) from the city centre, the museum commemorating those who died in this forested region is usually open only in summer, although tours can be arranged all year round (tel: 260 20 01).

ments. Other prominent Lithuanians, such as the painter, poet and composer **M. K. Čiurlionis** and the author and publicist **Jonas Basanavičius**, are also buried here.

Television Tower

The tallest building in the country, the 326m (1,071ft) **Television Tower** (Televizijos bokštas; open daily 10am–10pm; admission fee), is in the northeast suburb of Karoliniškės. On 13 January 1991, Soviet troops killed 14 unarmed civilians who were protesting against the Soviet regime here. A small space on the ground floor is dedicated to these men and women, with newspapers and black-and-white photographs.

At the top of the tower is the ever-so-slowly **revolving restaurant**, Paukščių Takas. The name means Bird Path, which in Lithuanian is also the name of the Milky Way. The restaurant affords a great view of the communist-era housing below and is one of the few non-smoking areas in town. Don't be alarmed if you see someone plummet from the building – bungee jumping takes place on some weekends *(see page 90)*.

Vingis Park

Situated to the west of the centre, in a loop of the Neris River, Vingis Park is the largest open space in the city. The outdoor **amphitheatre** is used for concerts and festivals during the warmer months. On the park's eastern edge is a **small cemetery** dedicated in 1918, in which Austrian, German, Polish and Russian soldiers are buried. A large statue of a felled lion commemorates all those who died in wars. There is also a small **botanical garden** (Botanikos sodas; tel: 231 79 33), run by Vilnius University, at the eastern end of the park near the river, but it can be viewed only by appointment.

EXCURSIONS

Trakai

If you make only one trip outside Vilnius, then make **Trakai** your destination. Once the country's capital and seat of power, it holds a special place in the Lithuanian psyche. Just 28km (17 miles) west of the city, it can be reached by frequent bus services, or the less frequent trains. By car, take Savanorių Street out of the city until it becomes the A4. The area is well signposted. Most tourists see only the castle, but the surrounding lakes, popular with the locals in summer, are worth a look too.

Trakai Castle sitting pretty in the midst of Lake Galvė

The town occupies a narrow peninsula between three lakes, by far the largest of which is **Lake Galvė**. Legend has it that the lake got its name (*galva* in Lithuanian means 'head') after Grand Duke Vytautas had decapitated an enemy and thrown his head into the lake, supposedly giving the lake an appetite for human heads.

Legend aside, the area's strategic importance made it a centre of conflict in medieval times between Lithuania and the Teutonic Knights. In the early 15th century, Grand Duke Vytautas selected a small island in Lake Galvė and on it built one of the strongest castles in Europe, now known as **Trakai Castle** (Island Castle). Walking across the drawbridge and

into the castle, with its great brick walls and fairytale towers, is one of the most spectacular experiences in Eastern Europe. Inside, the **Trakai Castle Museum** (Trakų pilies muziejus; open Tues–Sun 10am–6pm; closed Mon; admission fee) focuses on Vytautas, and describes the castle's history, including its destruction by the Russians in the 17th century and the 1950s movement to restore the ruined structure to its original glory. Among the castle buildings, the residential quarters are notable for their high ceilings and lake views.

In summer, sailing boats and windsailors take over the lake. If you feel like joining in, wander over to the edge of the bridge where the boats come ashore, and the boatmen will start negotiating prices with you.

Trakai shoreline

Back in town, part of Trakai's main street is named Karaimų, highlighting the town's Karaite heritage. The Karaites are a Turkic-speaking people from the Black Sea region who adhere to Karaism, a religion that incorporates elements of Judaism. Campaigning in the region in 1397, Vytautus the Great took many Karaite prisoners of war, and brought some of them to Trakai to serve as his personal bodyguards. Today, only 100 or so Karaites remain in the town, but their legacy lives on. Their brightly coloured timber houses line Karaimų, and at No. 30 stands the Kenesa, their prayer house. At No. 22, the **Karaite Ethnographic Museum** (Karaimų Etnografijos muziejus; open Wed–Sun 10am–6pm; closed Mon–Tues; admission fee) tells the community's story, using displays that range from weaponry and costumes to cooking utensils and jewellery. Before leaving, try a typical Karaite dish, *kibinai*, a meat-and-onion-filled pastry.

The island castle of Trakai was built by Grand Duke Vytautas

Close to Trakai castle on Lake Skaisčio, which is adjacent to Lake Galvė, is **Užutrakis palace** and manor. The palace and manor house have seen better days and are currently under renovation. The grounds, however, are a beautiful place to wander in and have a picnic. Nearby stables offer riding excursions through the surrounding countryside.

The Centre of Europe

A 1989 study by French cartographers found the physical centre of Europe to lie 25km (15 miles) outside Vilnius, a spot now marked by a fairly uninteresting park (see box on page 69). A much more worthwhile attraction that also pays tribute to this geographical fact is **Europe's Park** (Europos parkas; tel: 237 70 77; open daily 9am–sunset; admission fee), about 11km (7 miles) from the outskirts of the city. This sculpture park, established in 1991, covers nearly 55 hectares (136 acres) of wooded countryside. So far, more than 90 works by sculptors from around the world are on

Infotree **sculpture by Gintaras Karosas**

display. Among them is Gintaras Karosas' *LNK Infotree*, made up of 3,000 television sets arranged to create a winding path towards a decaying statue of Lenin. One of the most photographed and striking installations is Dennis Openheim's *Drinking Structure with Exposed Kidney Pool*, which looks a bit like a large gypsy caravan with an elephant's trunk. Other striking sculptures include Magdalena Abakanowicz's *Space of Unknown Growth*, which consists of a number of giant egg-like concrete boulders, and Jon Barlow Hudson's *Cloud Hands*, granite blocks that seem to hang in mid-air. At the northwest end of the park there is a small restaurant. At the **post office**, you can send postcards to friends bearing a Centre of Europe postmark.

Grūtas Park

Grūtas Park (Grūto Parkas; tel: 313 55 511; open Oct–Apr 9am–5pm, May–Sept 9am–8pm; admission fee) is a kind of retirement home for Soviet-era sculptures that were removed from cities and towns across the whole of Lithuania during the early 1990s. The park caused some controversy when it opened in 2001. Some people feel that it trivialises the country's Soviet history, although others feel the park can act as a teaching tool for future generations. Whatever its rights and wrongs, the park is unquestionably one of the strangest places in the country. A path leads through the forest, at first passing numerous statues from the Communist pantheon – Marx, Engels, Stalin, Lenin – and then Lithuanian worthies. On 1 April, actors dressed as Soviet-era personalities roam the grounds and entertain the crowd, mostly by poking fun at the Soviet government and the everyday life of its citizens. Lenin's birthday (22 April), Victory Day (9 May) and the October Revolution (7 November) are all celebrated here.

The park is so large that on days when it is not particularly busy one can feel very much alone. A small museum and picture gallery houses Soviet propaganda. There's also a children's playground and café.

The park is near the town of Druskininkai about 130km (80 miles) southwest of Vilnius. By car, take the A4 motorway from Vilnius. Buses also run from Vilnius to Druskininkai, but you'll need to walk for 1km (½-mile) from the bus stop to the park entrance.

The Centre of Europe

A group of French National Geographic Institute members 'discovered' the official physical centre of Europe in 1989. They deemed it to be 25km (15 miles) outside Vilnius, on the road to Molėtai. Europos Centras, a small park dedicated to this fact, is worth little more than a brief photo-stop. The spot is marked by a paved square surrounded by a series of European flags and a long column with EU stars shining above it. There is also a large boulder on to which people throw coins. In the one-room museum you can buy a certificate authenticating the fact that you have paid a visit to the Centre of Europe.

A rustic thatched-roof house typical of the Žemaitija region

Open-Air Museum of Lithuania

Explore the nation's rural past at the **Open-Air Museum of Lithuania** (Lietuvos Liaudies Buities Muziejus Rumšiškėse; tel: 346 473 92; open May–Oct 10am–6pm; closed Mon; admission fee includes map). Located at Rumšiškės, 20km (12 miles) outside Kaunas *(see page 72)* on the A1 motorway, this is the largest of its kind in the country, covering nearly 176 hectares (435 acres) of lovely countryside and featuring more than 150 buildings taken from all over Lithuania.

The museum is laid out in four village-like clusters, connected by a paved, circular path, 6.5km (4 miles) long. Each cluster represents one of the four regions of Lithuania – Žemaitija, Dzūkija, Aukštaitija and Suvalkija – and has buildings and settings that are typical of that area. The rustic wooden buildings include windmills, inns and churches, as well as farmhouses. To give a more realistic view of life in the 18th and 19th centuries, 50 or so buildings have been decked out with furniture, kitchen articles, decorations and work tools of a particular period and place.

During busier weekends or on days related to pagan beliefs (such as the summer solstice or Joninės on 24 June and Žolinė on 15 August), actors dressed as peasants or townsfolk perform traditional crafts such as furniture-making, pottery and weaving, and show the daily tasks of rural life. There are also horse-ploughing competitions and crafts markets throughout the summer season.

One area of the park is a recreation of a typical main square with buildings that serve as workshops for artisans, a great place to take children. Also good for younger visitors are the swings and see-saws sprinkled throughout the park. Boat rentals for trips along the Nemunas are available; ask for details and prices at the information office.

Two Traditions

As long ago as 9000BC, people are believed to have settled in Kernavė, a small village 24km (15 miles) north of Vilnius. Now partly preserved as a site of archaeological importance, this historic village is most notable for two annual traditions.

On the evening of 23 June, Midsummer *(Rasos)* is celebrated. During this, the shortest night of the year, girls from the village wear wreaths on their heads. Later these wreaths are surrounded with candles and set adrift on the River Neris. Traditionally, the further a wreath floats, the sooner a girl will be married. The sight of myriad candles being carried slowly downstream amid the dark forest is captivating.

The evening also witnesses a search for the fern 'blossom'. In pagan times this event was little more than a way for boys and girls to pair off in the woods. Promiscuity was not simply tolerated on this night, but sanctioned, and some still try to maintain the tradition. Large bonfires are lit and many enjoy a more than healthy amount of alcohol. Men and boys try to leap over the fires, with mixed results. The festivities continue throughout the night.

In July, the more edifying Days of Live Archaeology takes place, with a large festival celebrating the past. There are presentations of medieval craft, hunting and military traditions, along with food stalls.

Kaunas Town Hall

Kaunas

Some 100km (60 miles) north of Vilnius, **Kaunas**, is the second largest city in the country and is considered the most Lithuanian. Having acted as the interim capital between the wars, it is looked on as the bastion of Lithuanian culture.

The **Old Town** of Kaunas is similar to that of Vilnius, with an eclectic mixture of Gothic and Renaissance buildings, though the influence of baroque is not as strong as in the capital. Most of the city's main tourist attractions can be found around the long stretch of the pedestrian street of Vilniaus, which becomes Laisvės aleja. In the 13th century this road linked Vilnius and Kaunas. Today, the street begins at **Town Hall Square** (Rotušės aikštė), which was laid out in the early 16th century and is still surrounded by merchants' houses dating from that time. Dominating the centre of the square is the gigantic white Town Hall (Rotušė), which was first constructed in 1542 but now boasts mainly baroque and neoclassical elements including the wedding-cake style tower. In 1970, indeed, the Town Hall became the city's Wedding Palace, and parades and ceremonies involving up to 50 couples take place here every Saturday morning. The Town Hall also houses a small **Ceramics Museum** (tel: 20 35 72; open Tues–Sun

11am–5pm; closed Mon; admission fee), which displays finds from archaeological digs in the area.

At Rotušės No. 19 is the **History of Communication Museum** (Ryšių istorijos muziejus; open Wed–Thu 10am–6pm, Sat–Sun 10am–5pm; closed Mon, Tues, Fri; admission fee). Untranslated letters penned by Grand Duke Gediminas may not grab everyone's attention but the antique stamps and telephones might. Also of note on the square is the baroque **Church of St Francis Xavier and Jesuit Monastery** (Šv

Flying High

Aviators Steponas Darius and Stasys Girėnas are Lithuanian national heroes. After World War I, they emigrated to America and here they purchased a second-hand plane, which they named *Lituanica*, planning a flight from New York to Kaunas.

On 14 July 1932, as the two prepared for take off, a cable came in warning of a storm moving north across Europe. To add to the flight's perilous conditions, the pair hadn't secured permission from all the territories on their flight path. But these dangers were ignored.

The pilots' last communication was received in Newfoundland, although the bright orange plane was seen along the Polish and German borders. On 16 July, wreckage was discovered in a forest outside Soldin. Some concluded that the plane had been shot down by Germans, but this was ruled out by forensic evidence. Either stormy weather grounded the plane or the two men were simply exhausted after 37 hours of flight. At the time, numerous memorial services took place and there's little doubt that the disputed circumstances of their demise added to the myth surrounding them.

The remains of the *Lituanica* are housed in the Military Museum at Donelaičio 64 and a 23m- (75ft-) tall bronze monument stands in front of the football stadium, named in their honour, at Sporto and Perkūno. They also appear on the 10 Lt banknote *(see page 20)*.

Pranciškaus Ksavero bažnyčia ir Jėzuitų vienuolynas), which dates from the late 17th century.

The charming pedestrian, cobblestoned **Vilniaus gatvė** (Vilnius Street) intersects the northeast corner of the square and leads into **Laivės aleja** (Laisvės Boulevard), known for its broad walkway and variety of shops and monuments. Off Vilniaus is Zamenhofo Street, in which No. 12 houses **P. Stulga's Folk Music Museum** (tel: 42 22 95; open 10am–5pm; closed Mon–Tues; admission fee). On display here are various traditional Lithuanian instruments, including the *kanklės*, a trapezoidal-shaped piece of wood with string attached.

The city's residents like to stroll along Laivės aleja whose shops, restaurants, cafés and bars make for good browsing and carousing. Make a detour through the small **City Garden** (Miesto Sodas) to see the small memorials to Lithuanian partisans and other national heroes, including **Romas Kalanta**, a student who burned himself to death here in protest against the Soviet system on 14 May 1972. Opposite the City Garden, a statue of Grand Duke Vytautus stands over four defeated enemies: a Polish soldier, a Tatar, a Crusader and a Russian who bears a passing resemblance to a certain Vladimir Ilyich Lenin.

Walking north on Maironio from Laisvės leads into Putvinskio Street. The **Devil Museum** (Velnių muziejus; Putvinskio 64, tel: 22 15 87; open 11am–5pm; closed Mon; admission fee) is one of the strangest museums in the country. Its 2,000 devil carvings, toys, sculptures and masks grew from the collection of the Lithuanian painter and eccentric Antanas Žmuidzinavičius (1876–1966). Among the highlights are the Hitler and Stalin devils dancing joyfully on the body of Lithuania.

Laivės aleja's eastern side ends in **Independence Square** (Nepriklausomybės aikštė), which is dominated by the **Church of St Michael the Archangel** built in the 1890s by the Russians. The Catholic cathedral has a distinctive Byzantine flavour, which has caused many of the city's residents to refer to it as *soboras*, a Lithuanianisation of the Russian *sobor*, meaning cathedral. Absolutely breathtaking on a sunny day, the silver-coloured domes and blue exterior can be seen from half-way down Laisvės aleja. On warm weekends the entrance to the church is cluttered with newly married couples having their photographs taken.

Opposite the church is the **Mykolas Žilinskas Art Museum** (open 11am–5pm; closed Mon; admission fee), which has an impressive collection of paintings from the 17th to 20th centuries, including Lithuania's only Reubens. In front is a sculpture of the Greek god Nike by Petras Mazuras, erected in 1991. The statue's frank nudity embarrassed some of the city's more demure residents; the crane operator hired to place the statue here walked off the job when he saw it.

Strolling along Laivės Boulevard, with the Church of St Michael the Archangel in the distance

National Parks, Inland and on the Coast

Pagan Lithuanians took good care of their forests, which they considered sacred, creating a strong bond between the people and the land that has continued to the present day. This inherent respect for the nation's natural environment means that preservation of the four national parks is easier here than in many other countries. The Soviet occupation and the postwar drive for industrialisation did leave a few scars on nature, however, and the government is making continued efforts to undo any damage.

Two national parks are located in the northeast of the country, one in the southwest and one in the east. As well as protecting flora and fauna, each park incorporates villages and plays a role in maintaining the distinctive culture of its region.

Approximately 100km (62 miles) northeast of Vilnius lies the 40,570-hectare (100,270-acre) **Aukštaitija Nation-**

Aukštaitija National Park is made up of myriad interconnected lakes

al Park, made up of more than **200 interconnected lakes** and the land between them. About 70 percent of the land is covered by conifer forest, and there is a great diversity of flora and fauna, including red deer, roe deer, wild boar and, a more rarely glimpsed inhabitant, beaver. Canoe trips through this breathtaking glaciated landscape are popular, and there is no shortage of secluded campsites along the lake shores.

Wooden belfry at Palūšė

There are numerous villages within the park, the outstanding one being **Palūšė**, which has an 18th-century circular wooden church. Also within the park is the **Bee-keeping Museum** (Stripeikiai village, open daily May–mid-Oct 10am–7pm; closed mid-Oct–Apr; admission fee), where bee-keeping is explained and honey can be tasted. A map is absolutely essential for navigating through the area and can be obtained from the Aukštaitija National Park Authority (<www.ignalina.lt>).

In 1991 an area about 100km (62 miles) southwest of Vilnius near the Belarus border was designated the **Dzūkija National Park** (<www.dzukijosparkas.lt>). Situated in the basin of the Nemunas River, the 55,000-hectare (135,850-acre) area is mostly pine forests dotted with a few small villages. There are tourist information offices at two of them: Marcinkonys (Miškininkų 61, tel: 310 444 66) and **Merkinė** (Vilniaus 2, tel: 310 572 45). The latter, which stands at the confluence of the rivers Nemunas and Merkys,

Folk totem, Dzūkija National Park

is one of the oldest settlements in Lithuania, dating back to the 14th century. Tsar Peter the Great stayed here and Vladislav Vaza, the king of Poland, fell ill and died here in 1648. The historic village has a hill fort and a 17th-century church, which amalgamates Gothic and baroque.

The park is known for its abundance of mushrooms and in the autumn it is rare not to see a granny or two out in the woods digging for boletus or chanterelles. Unless you're adept at telling harmful and edible species apart, however, it's best to leave gathering mushrooms to the locals. The area is also famous for its berries, which in summer seem to spring up on every bush. Accommodation in the park ranges from camping sites to homesteads to bed-and- breakfast. Expect humble yet cosy surroundings.

The **Curonian Spit National Park** (Kuršių Nerijos Nacionalinis Parkas; <www.nerija.lt>), in the northeast, is the country's only coastal park. It protects the precious sliver of sand – no more than 1.5km (1 mile) wide and 60m (200ft) high – separating the Curonian lagoon from the Baltic Sea. Winds formed the long, narrow spit 5,000 years ago, making this geologically the youngest part of the country. With white, sandy hills and pine forests set against the dark blue sea, this is a spellbinding place. To get there, take the A1 motorway from Vilnius to **Klaipėda** and then a ferry over to the spit. The coastal town of **Palanga**, about 20km (12 miles) from

Klaipėda, is Lithuania's favourite beach resort, its population increasing five-fold during the brief summer season.

Northern Lithuania takes in the Samogitian or Žemaitija region. An undoubted highlight is the **Hill of Crosses** 12km (8 miles) outside the city of Šiauliai, which is northeast of Vilnius along the A2 then A9 motorways. Over the past two centuries pilgrims have planted thousands upon thousands of crosses of all shapes and sizes, completely covering a small hill – an amazing sight. Also in this part of the country is **Žemaitija National Park** (<www.zemaitijosnp.lt>), which has beautiful Lake Plateliai as its focus. The park also includes a number of cultural attractions, including the pilgrimage village of Žemaičių Kalvarija. An information office in the village of Plateliai (Didžioji 10; tel: 448 492 31) is located 22km (13½ miles) north of the town of Plungė. Camping is allowed but only in a small area.

Žemaitijan living room

WHAT TO DO

ENTERTAINMENT

Productions and shows in Vilnius are geared to local audiences and little effort is made to cater for foreigners. Most visitors who wish to explore serious entertainment will opt for a classical music concert or opera.

The **National Philharmonic Hall**, the country's premier concert hall (Aušros Vartų 5; tel: 266 52 16; <www.filharmonija.lt>), hosts many national and international concerts. There is a cosier atmosphere at the classical music concerts held in **St Johns' Church** in the Vilnius University complex on most Sunday evenings at about 6pm. Check outside the church door for information.

National Drama Theatre poster

Other venues in the city include the **National Drama Theatre** (tel: 262 97 71; <www.teatras.lt>), the **Opera and Ballet Theatre** (tel: 262 07 27; <www.opera.lt>), the **Russian Drama Theatre** (tel: 262 71 33), the **Vilnius Congressional Palace** (tel: 261 88 28; <www.lvso.lt>), the **Vilnius Great Theatre** (tel: 273 70 78; <www.dvt.lt>) and the **Vilnius Small Theatre** (tel: 261 31 95; <www.vmt.lt>).

Small-scale events take place at **M. K. Čiurlionis Museum house** (tel: 212 64 14) and the **Vilnius Music Academy** (tel: 261 26 91), which showcases its young and

Cyclists at Trakai, also a popular location for swimming and sailing

One of Vilnius' chic drinking establishments

undiscovered talents. The **Youth Theatre** (tel: 261 61 26), holds similar events for young actors and actresses.

The **Concert and Sports Palace** (Rinktinės 1; tel: 272 89 42) stages larger concerts and hosts the occasional visiting circus. Plans to renovate or demolish the building are at hand. A new **Siemens Arena** (Ozo 14) is under construction in the northwest section of the city. In summer many concerts, from classical to heavy metal, take place in **Vingis Park's amphitheatre**. The best place for information about all events is the Vilnius Tourist Information Centre (Vilniaus 22; tel: 26 29 660; fax: 262 81 69; <www.turizmas.vilnius.lt>).

Nightlife

Central Vilnius – especially the Old Town – has a wide range of nightlife to explore, from stylish designer bars to raucous nightclubs. Many are open into the early hours of the morning. If you feel like a bit of variety on your night out but don't want to walk from venue to venue, a number of hotels on the northern side of the river have a nightclub, bar and casino under the one roof. Any time before midnight is a good time to visit one of the many beer tents that spring up along Pilies or Vokiečių in the summer. Later in the evening most patrons move inside, or on to some of the city's clubs.

Although the crime rate is not high, visitors out on the town should be aware of their personal belongings at all times and should stick to well-lit areas walking home. For the most up-to-date bar and club information pick up a copy of *Vilnius In Your Pocket* or log on to the website, <www.inyourpocket.com>.

SHOPPING

Where to Shop

A walk down virtually any street in the Old Town confronts the visitor with innumerable souvenir and craft shops selling everything from amber to woodcarvings. Try the outdoor craft market at the junction of Pilies and Didžioji to find similar items at slightly lower prices; Žydų and Stiklių streets are also worth looking around. Clothing and shoe shops are concentrated along Gedimino Avenue in the New Town. The Europa Centre (Konstitucijos 7a), in a landmark building north of the river, has a modern shopping mall. The antiques quarter is along Dominikonų Street beside Vilnius University.

Modern shopping mall near Green Bridge

Art stall, Pilies Street

For local colour (and bargains), nothing beats a market. The largest is at Gariūnai, about 4km (2½ miles) west of the city centre along the A1. Just about everything can be found here: cars, food, household goods, kitchen ware, wigs, tools, wedding dresses and much more. The magic of this place lies in its intensity and the people-watching opportunities that go with it. Kalvarijų market, across the river in the northern suburb of Šnipiškės, is a smaller version with a less arresting variety of goods, though occasionally a rummage can produce some exceptionally good Soviet-made cameras and lenses. At the weekends from 10am–3pm the building at Pamėnkalinio 7 plays host to a CD and DVD market. A flower market at Basanavičiaus 42 is open 24 hours. All markets are closed on Mondays and open from sunrise to mid-afternoon unless otherwise noted. Pick-pockets target these markets, so be especially alert when moving through large crowds.

What to Buy

Handmade wooden chests, delicate glassware, farmhouse bric-a-brac and Russian religious icons are among the wares you will find in the city's **antiques** shops. If you're serious about buying, be aware that if any of the pieces are more than 50 years old, a duty of 10–20 percent must be paid before going through customs at the airport *(see page 110 for more information)*.

Clothing ranges from folk to funky, conservative to cutting-edge. The retail giant Apranga (there's a branch in the

Europa Centre mall) sells a variety of clothing from all over Europe and has a few well-know Baltic designer lines, too. Two large Lithuanian clothing companies are Audimas, known for its sportswear, and Utenos trikotažas, which specialises in soft cotton underwear for men, women and children. For sports fans a great souvenir to take home is a Žalgiris basketball jersey.

For more individualistic designs, the *madinga* (fashionable) shopper might want to visit a more upmarket outlet. Nijolė at Gedimino 2 has large range of fur coats. In the Old Town, Ramunė Piekautaitė's shop at Didžioji 20 has classic styles for women, while Yzzy at Gaono 10 is aimed at a younger market. Other one-of-a-kind creations can be found at Zoraza (Stiklių 6).

Practical and attractive, Lithuanian-made **linen** *(linas)* – everything from napkins and doilies to bedding and table-

All kinds of linen products are available, including smart jackets

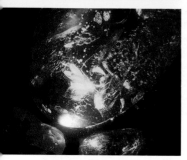

Amber can be bought in the city in numerous forms

cloths – is an excellent buy. Shops and stalls all over the city sell linen, with the biggest concentration of outlets around Pilies Street. Prices of embroidered articles vary significantly depending on whether the embroidery is hand-sewn or machined. Bring bed or table measurements with you.

Linen folk costumes are an ever-popular purchase. A *juosta*, a brilliantly embroidered sash, makes a good souvenir. These vary from a bookmark to a table runner in size, and were traditionally given as gifts or made to commemorate a special occasion, such as a wedding or birthday. The embroided design often incorporates a name (such as 'Lietuva', or Lithuania) or a folk saying.

Lithuania is the source of much of the **amber** in the Baltics, making Vilnius the ideal hunting ground for lovers of this gem-like substance *(see opposite)*.

Lithuania produces a number of **alcoholic beverages** that are virtually impossible to find outside the country; they are also cheap by international standards. Alita sparkling wine, produced since 1980, makes a good purchase. Among the nation's liqueurs are the very sweet Bobelinė and Palanga, and those infused with fruits or grasses and roots such as Starka, Medžiotojų, along with mead-based Balzamas, Trejos devynerios, Suktinis and Žalgiris. Rye-based Samanė is also good. Be aware that the duty-free shops in the airport are small. The best selection and prices can be found in the city's grocery shops.

Music makes a distinctive souvenir. The largest label in the country is Garsų Pasaulis (Pamėnkalnio 14; tel: 262 25 51; <www.gpi.lt>) and their shop on a street which is the northern extension of Pylimo is well stocked with Lithuanian recordings, including folk and choral music. Muzikos bomba (Jakšto 24; tel: 262 45 47), off Gedimino, stocks jazz,

Amber

A celebrated folk tale holds that amber, or *gintaras*, was created when Jūratė, a beautiful mermaid, fell in love with Kastytis, a simple fisherman, and took him to her amber castle under the Baltic Sea. Unhappy at this arrangement, the god Perkūnas sent a storm to rend the castle asunder, leaving the fragments to wash up on the shore. Pieces of amber shaped as teardrops are said to be those of the lamenting goddess.

Science, however, tells a different story. Baltic amber is resin, emitted from the bark of trees, which has hardened and fossilised over the course of around 30–40 million years. Sometimes insects or leaves were caught in the ooze and amber with these are called inclusions. It is rare to find this kind of amber sold in shops in Vilnius.

Numerous types of amber exist. Often the classification is by colour. In Vilnius you can find white, yellow, orange/red and green amber. White amber, or king's amber, is usually off-white with some yellow accents. Similarly, yellow amber is typically yellow with swathes of white throughout. The orange/red varieties are the most common and green amber is the rarest, commanding a higher price. Authentic amber shouldn't float in seawater or turn to powder when scraped with a knife. Unfortunately, no right-minded street vendor will allow you to test this.

Most amber is converted into jewellery, polished or left natural and strung as necklaces or inlaid with silver, or made into rings or bracelets. Houseware, such as glasses and cups, with amber decoration is becoming more popular. The two best streets to search for amber are Pilies and Aušros Vartų.

A woodworker's workshop

classical, folk, pop and other genres by Lithuanian and international artists. The best place to find independent and rare secondhand CDs and records is in the Old Town at Thelonious (Stiklių 12; tel: 22 10 76; <www.thelonious.lt>).

Woodcarving has a long tradition in this heavily forested country, and a vast range of products is produced, running all the way from decorative pieces of cutlery and crucifixes to devil masks and small toys such as duck-shaped whistles. Look also for beautifuly woven wicker baskets and handicrafts made from flax or straw.

SPORTS

Inevitably, given the country's cold climate, the favourite sports tend to be of the indoor kind. Balancing this, however, is the locals' delight in (summer) outdoors recreation, taking advantage of the city's hinterland of forest, lake and farmland.

Spectator Sports

Basketball is the national pastime, and the ups and downs of clubs cause heated debate between hardcore fans. The Lithuanian team, which regularly tops the European championships, is a source of great national pride The best-known club is the Kaunas-based Žalgiris, but the Vilnius Lietuvos Rytas has begun to make a name for itself outside the country. To see a Žalgiris Kaunas game requires a drive to Kaunas' Darius and

Girėnas Sports Complex (Perkūno 3; tel: 37 20 14 70). The Lietuvos Rytas club's stadium is more accessible; contact the stadium for ticket sales (Olimpiečių 3; tel: 272 18 45).

Football is also a popular, with games often televised in bars and pubs. The season runs from April to November.

Participation Sports

By far the best way to stay active in Lithuania is by **cycling** through the countryside or **swimming** or **canoeing** through the numerous lakes to the city's north or around Trakai to the southwest. For information about national parks, see page 76 or contact the Vilnius Tourist Information centres at either Vilniaus 22 (tel: 26 29 660; fax: 262 81 69) or the Town Hall (tel: 262 64 70; fax: 262 07 62).

It's natural that winter sports are popular in these parts. Although not always the safest option, **sledding** on the city's

Boating on Lake Galvė, Trakai

hills is popular. The lack of mountains ensures that **skiing** is only of the cross-country variety. **Ice rinks** are located in the shopping complex Akropolis (Ozo 25; tel: 248 48 48) north-west of the city centre, or at the Ice Palace (Ąžuolyno 9; tel: 24 24 212) in the northwest suburb of Viršuliškės, which is open to the public at different times, depending on whether the Vilnius city hockey team is using the facilities for practice.

Go-karting (Savanorių 178; tel: 23 11 507) is one of the more popular pastimes. **Bowling** has also taken off. Bowling alleys include the small but pleasant Boulingo Klubas (Jasinskio 16; tel: 24 96 600), the spacious and modern Cosmic Bowling Centre (Vytenio 6; tel: 23 39 909) and Ten Pin (Žirmūnų 68; tel: 27 70 760). **Bungee jumping** from the Television Tower happens at weekends. Contact the Latvia-based LGK company (tel: 600 23 210; <www.atrakcionai.lt>) for more details.

CHILDREN

By far the most exciting place for children within the city will be any of the outdoor festivals *(see page 92)*. During summer the occasional carnival or circus will come through town. For

> **Children are welcome at many cafés and restaurants, and it is not uncommon to see parents enjoy their dinner while their children either nod off under the table or play quietly in a corner. They tend not to be coddled or otherwise patronised, and are left on their own to play or amuse themselves.**

more subdued entertainment, the Lėlė Puppet Theatre (Arklių 5; tel: 262 86 78) has adorable shows that will engage younger guests despite language barriers.

The Open-Air Museum of Lithuania in Rumšiškės *(see page 70)* is an engaging way to learn something about farm life and rural crafts. It also has some enticing swings and see-saws. Grūtas

Colourful hobby horses for sale in the Old Town

Park *(see page 68)* may teach them something about communism – and they can enjoy the play equipment there, too. A boat trip along Lake Galvė in Trakai could also prove fun.

There is a small petting zoo, Pavilnys (Džiaugsmo 44; tel: 267 48 73), outside the city, but opening times can be erratic so it is best to call ahead. The only real zoo in the country is in Kaunas' Ąžuolynas Park (tel: 33 25 40; open Apr–Sep 9am–7pm, Oct–Mar 9am–5pm; admission fee) and it is not particularly remarkable.

Once winter snow is firmly in place many of the city's hills are taken over by kids intent on sledding, using everything from cardboard boxes to fancy factory-made sleds. Indoor activities such as ice skating are another option *(see page 90)*. If all else fails, take them to the mall. Both the city's large shopping centres, Akropolis (Ozo 25; tel: 248 48 48) and Europa (Konstitucijos 7a; tel: 248 70 70), have play areas for children.

FESTIVALS

The Vilnius year is punctuated by a large number of small festivals. For an up-to-date listing with precise dates of events contact the Vilnius Tourist Information office. The popular Lithuanian Song Festival takes place every four years in the first week of July; the next one is scheduled for 2007.

Many festivals blend pagan and Christian celebrations. Before the beginning of Lent, Shrovetide or *Užgavėnės* celebrations take place in the city's streets. People wear costumes and masks, and in the evening a large effigy of a woman, symbolising winter, is burned. The patron saint of Lithuania is St Casimir and on the weekend closest to his feast day (4 March) a large fair called Kaziukas takes place in the Old Town. Almost everyone on the streets that day will be buying, selling or walking around carrying *verbos*, a long stick of colourful dried flowers, grasses and/or herbs. The *verbos* are used later as makeshift palm fronds for Palm Sunday services. Folk art and sugary treats are sold at stalls on this day.

On 1 November, All Saints' Day is celebrated, while the day after is *Vėlinės*, a pagan holiday. Both commemorate the dead and have been melded together, often with both names being used interchangeably. Because 1 November is a national holiday, most people use the day to visit graves and set candles around them. The bonfire ceremony at Rasų Cemetery, by the grave of Polish General Józef Piłsudski's heart, is particularly atmospheric.

Girls playing *kanklės* (a kind of harp) at the Song Festival

Calendar of Events

1 January New Year's celebrations throughout the city.

6 January A recreation of the three Magis' visit to the Christ child takes place on Cathedral Square.

16 February Independence Day.

26–27 February *Užgavėnės*, a Shrovetide celebration, takes place in the Old Town on the weekend before Lent.

4 March Feast of St Casimir, the patron saint of Lithuania. A large fair in the Old Town is held on the first weekend of the month.

May International Folklore Festival concentrates mostly on music.

June Vilnius Festival celebrates classical music in many of the city's venues and is overseen by the Vilnius Philharmonic.

23 June Midsummer, or *Rasos*. Events take place in Vilnius, but Kernavė hosts a far more traditional festival *(see page 71)*.

24 June Feast Day of St John, *Joninės*, continues the midsummer festivities.

July St Christopher Festival is a large music festival that takes place in various venues throughout the city.

6 July Mindaugas Coronation Day. A national holiday; a large festival takes place in Kernavė.

15 August *Žolinė*, or the Feast of the Assumption, is a public holiday and sees many small activities throughout the city. At Rumšiškės, the Open-Air Museum of Lithuania also hosts a celebration.

September Vilnius City Festival: a week of fireworks and carnivals; the Vilnius Jazz Festival also takes place.

September–October Old Music Festival with medieval and baroque church music played in many of the city's churches.

1 November All Saints' Day sees many of the city's residents visiting cemeteries and placing candles around the graves of deceased relatives. At Rasų Cemetery, ethnic Polish Lithuanians light a bonfire at the grave of General Józef Piłsudski's heart.

23 December–5 January Numerous concerts, mostly dedicated to church music, are held throughout the city. A Christmas tree lighting ceremony takes place on Cathedral Square.

EATING OUT

Lithuanian food is decidedly heavy. Main dishes are typically meat (usually pork) with potatoes and cabbage. Vegetables, unfortunately, tend to be boiled or fried within an inch of their lives; salads are almost always a better option, although they tend to be appetisers rather than a main dish. Most visitors will find restaurant meals quite inexpensive. A three-course meal per person without alcohol should cost between 40 and 90 Lt.

For a change from local fare, try the ever-increasing number of ethnic restaurants. For some reason, Chinese restaurants are particularly numerous. *(For listings, see page 136.)*

WHERE TO EAT

Summers in the Baltics are short, so most residents eat outside at the first sign of warmth. Outdoor tables and chairs are not brought in until restaurateurs and their patrons reluctantly admit that summer is coming to a close.

Restaurants and cafés are concentrated in the Old Town and city centre. Because these are tourist areas most have an English-language menu. Often the staff will speak some English, especially if they are under the age of 25. Gracious but unsuccessful attempts at the Lithuanian language will usually be met with smiles and then a switch to English or German.

Note that restaurants often put a reserved *(rezervuota)* sign on a table to keep people from lingering too long over a cup of coffee, so don't be put off if the restaurant seems to be booked out.

Often, mineral water *(mineralinis vanduo)* is described conversationally as *su burbuliukais* (with bubbles, or sparkling), and *be burbuliukų* (without bubbles, or still).

Café society in the Old Town

WHAT TO EAT

Soups tend to be hearty and almost always come with a few floating pieces of potato. In summer, a popular soup made from beets *(šaltibarščiai)* is served cold with warm potatoes on the side topped with sour cream and dill. A warm version, *barščiai*, is served year-round. Another option is sorrel soup *(rūgštynių sriuba)*, made from a beef stock and vegetables with tons of the tangy herb. The Lithuanian national dish is considered by most to be *cepelinai* (zeppelins), which take their name from their blimp-like shape. These potato dumplings are stuffed with a mixture of ground beef and pork or just pork. They usually come in pairs and sometimes are not just boiled but also fried, making them very filling.

Vegetable garnishes to traditional main courses are usually beet, cabbage and/or carrot sometimes soaked in vinegar. Mushrooms grow wild throughout most of the country and collecting them is a national pastime, so they find their way into many of the soups and sauces. Starchy dishes, usually potato-based, are ubiquitous. Dough made from curd, or baker's cheese *(varškėčiai)* is used in both sweet and savoury dishes. Potato dumpling *(kugelis)* and potato pancakes *(bulviniai blynai)* along with pancakes *(lietiniai)* stuffed with vegetables or meat can be found in almost all the city's establishments offering Lithuanian dishes. Ravioli *(koldūnai)* are stuffed with pork and served without a sauce. Bread comes with almost every meal and ranges from thin white slices to the dark hearty rye varieties, a few slices of which can feel like a meal in itself.

Pasty restaurant sign

Fish

The Baltic Sea is, unfortunately, largely fished-out, which is why river or lake fish are more readily available and often significantly cheaper than saltwater fish. Carp *(karpis)* is the traditional main course during the Christmas holidays. It is often purchased live, taken home and put in the bath until it meets its end later in the day. Pike *(lydeka)* is also common. Herring *(silkė)* is served cold and as a starter with either a sour cream sauce or vinaigrette dressing. Eels *(ungurys)* are common in Lithuania's lakes and are often smoked.

Meat

A plethora of pork products can be found throughout the Baltics. A Lithuanian variation is *skilandis*, made of spiced ground pork placed usually in a stomach but sometimes a bladder and then smoked. *Karbonadas* is another popular dish. This is a chunk of pork rolled in bread crumbs, then in egg, then fried.

Cold beetroot soup is served during the summer months

Sausages *(dešrelės)* are also a big part of the culinary tradition and tend not to be spicy. Potato 'sausages' *(vėdarai)* are pig intestines filled with grated potatoes. Another potato and meat combination is *Žemaičių blynai* (Žemaitija pancakes), which are made from mashed potato-dough filled with boiled meat and then fried. And in case you want cabbage, too, then pickled stewed cabbage with potatoes and sausages *(troškinti rauginti kopūstai su bulvėmis ir dešrelėmis)* should do the trick. Cabbage leaves stuffed with meat and rice *(balandėliai)* are also popular. Local wild boar is a rare treat found at some of the city's traditional Lithuanian establishments.

Vegetarian Cuisine

Although Balti Drambliai *(see page 137)* is the only wholly vegetarian restaurant in Vilnius, there are still plenty of vegetarian options in what seems like a meat-and-potato world. Most of the city's eateries have salads on offer and dishes such as potato pancakes *(bulviniai blynai)* or pancakes *(lietiniai)* stuffed with mushrooms, cheese or both. Less common are potato dumplings *(švilpikai)*, sometimes called potato puffs

The forests of Dzūkija National Park are rich in wild mushrooms

or pads, which are either baked or boiled. Vegetarians should be aware that dishes described as 'with vegetables' *(su daržovėmis)* can still contain meat, poultry or fish, so check before ordering. Soups will hardly ever have a vegetarian stock or base, with the exception of the cold beet soup *(šaltibarščiai)*, which is served only during the warmer months of the year. Establishments catering for visitors will almost always have at least one if not several vegetarian main courses. Vegans will for the most part have to resort to eating salads with vinegar-based dressings for the duration of their stay.

Desserts

Those with a sweet tooth are well catered for in Vilnius. Among the local delicacies are numerous types of buns *(pyragėliai)*, cakes *(pyragas)* and doughnuts *(spurgos)*. A popular ingredient in cakes is poppy seeds, and a slice of poppy-seed cake *(pyragas su aguonomis)* makes a popular dessert. Towering honey cakes *(meduolis)* can be seen in the windows of most bakeries and come in two basic varieties: soft *(minkštas meduolis)* and the regular. Another common cake, *šakotis*, similar to the German *baumkuchen*, measures about 1m (3ft) in height and is shaped like a tree. The yellow colour is produced by the large number of egg yolks that go into making it. Another dessert of note is cranberry pudding *(spanguolių kisielius)* with a sweet and tangy taste.

Meal Times

Most hotels include breakfast in the price of the room. Breakfast is not commonly served in cafés and restaurants, but many of the city's establishments open their doors early for anyone wanting a pork loin and mashed potatoes to start their day. For lighter options head to a *kavinė* (café) or bakery *(kepykla)*. Finding a meal outside regular lunch hours (11am–1pm) or dinner hours (6–9pm) will not cause too much difficulty, at least to those in the Old Town or centre. Most restaurants serve food throughout the day and into the early hours of the morning.

Snacks and Light Meals

For light meals head into any of the city's cafés, bakeries or milk bars *(pieno baras)*. Milk bars, a fast-disappearing feature of the culinary landscape, sell baked goods, coffee and tea. Bakeries will serve much more than baked goods. You'll find pancakes *(lietiniai* or *blyneliai)* stuffed with meat, vegetables or sometimes even sweet jams or cheese. A café will have a greater variety of dishes

Finding non-smoking cafés or restaurants in Vilnius is a well-nigh impossible task. The smoking and non-smoking sections of restaurants often seem to be arbitrary, and smoking tables will be adjacent to non-smoking ones. Two places in the Old Town are completely smoke-free: Balti Drambliai or White Elephants (Vilniaus 41; open Mon–Fri 11am–12am, Sat–Sun noon–12am), and the old-style Lithuanian restaurant in the Old Town, Gabi (Šv Mykolo 6; open 11am–10pm).

than a bakery and is less likely to be self-service. Those looking for healthy options should study the salad section of a menu. Spicy salad (*pikantiškos salotos*) is simply a mixture of cheese, hard-boiled eggs and mayonnaise topped with garlic.

Places selling light meals line Pilies and Gedimino. Two outstanding eateries are located outside these hotspots. **My Café** (Mano kavinė; Bokšto 7; tel: 215 30 00; open daily 11am–last guest), in the Old Town, has an almost cult following for its rich variety of teas and tasty array of salads, soups and pancakes augmented by large main courses. Another popular haunt is the **Užupis Café** (Užupio kavinė; Užupio 2; tel: 212 21 38; open daily 10am–11pm), which has a lovely patio along the Vilnia River and a lively atmosphere thanks to its regular clientele of alternative types from the local Užupis scene.

Beer

Lithuanians take their *alus* (beer) seriously. Many first-time visitors are surprised by how light, refreshing and inexpensive many of the local brews are. The main brands are Horn Kalnapilis, Žvyturys, Utenos and Tauras. Beer is usually drunk with a light snack known as a 'beer set' (*rinkinys prie alaus*). The most common is *kepta duona*, pieces of dark bread deep-fried and accompanied by a massive amount of garlic. Some enjoy it *su sūriu*, with cheese melted on top. Other snacks range from the mundane peanuts (*žemės riešutai*) to the more acquired taste of smoked pig's ears (*rūkytos kiaulių ausys*), pig's trotter (*kiaulės koja*), dried meats similar to jerky (*basturma*) and beef tongue (*jautienos liežuvis*). Less colourful options include cheese sticks (*sūrio lazdelės*) and mashed peas with smoked fat (*žirnių košė*). A wide variety of herring (*silkė*) is consumed, too, but usually only when vodka is being imbibed.

Drinks

Gira is a light, fermented drink that is easy on the foreign palate. It is similar to Russian *kvass* and sometimes the names are used interchangeably. Most types of *gira* are made either from bread or caraway seeds, with a few varieties made from fermented barley, cranberries or even honey. In some of the more traditional establishments *gira* is served with raisins floating in it. For something a bit stronger, try

Lithuanian spirits

Palanga and *Bobelinė,* both made from cranberries. Their strong, saccharine flavour makes them taste somewhat medicinal. In fact, *Bobelinė* was for years advertised as a tonic with rejuvenating powers.

Mead-based spirits, flavoured with herbs and other additives, are also commonly drunk. One of the more popular varieties, *Trejos Devynerios* ('three times nine'), is made with 27 grasses, blossoms, leaves and roots. *Balzamas* is a mead whose dark colour gives a hint of its effects should too much be imbibed. *Suktinis* is a lighter version of the same drink.

Spiking tea is a common practice. One of the best accompaniments to tea is *Starka,* a fruit-based liqueur, or *Medžiotojų,* 'the hunter's spirit', made from herbs. The taste of both is quite smooth.

Certain types of local liqueur are very high in alcohol and should be tried only if one's constitution is strong or sense of adventure insatiable. *Samanė* is made from rye and if tried in

Beer and *kepta duona*, fried garlic bread

the countryside can be exceedingly high in alcohol as it is made as a sort of moonshine. The type that can be bought in shops has an alcohol content of around 40 percent. The notorious *Žalgiris* mead is as powerful as the Kaunas basketball team of the same name, with an alcohol content hovering around 75 percent.

Of the few wines made in the country, all are forgettable. Alita, the locally produced sparkling wine ('champagne'), is more palatable.

To Help You Order ...

May I have a menu?	**Galima meniu?**
Can I have this without …?	**Ar galima be … ?**
I am a vegetarian.	**Aš esu vegetaras.**
The bill, please.	**Prašau sąskaitą.**
	(or **Galima sąskaitą?**)
I would like …	**Aš noriu …**

beer	**alus**	ice cream	**ledai**
bread	**duona**	the menu	**meniu**
butter	**sviestas**	milk	**pienas**
cheese	**sūris**	salad	**salotos**
coffee	**kava**	sugar	**cukrus**
dessert	**desertas**	tea	**arbata**
eggs	**kiaušiniai**	wine	**vynas**

... and Read the Menu

agurkai	cucumbers	**morkos**	carrots
aštrus	spicy	**obuoliai**	apple
apelsinai	orange	**padažas**	sauce
baklažanai	aubergine	**paštetas**	pâté
bananai	banana	**paukštiena**	poultry
brokoliai	broccoli	**peletrūnas**	tarragon
bulviniai	potato	**pomidorai**	tomatoes
blynai	pancakes	**pupelės**	beans
burokėliai	beets	**ryžiai**	rice
česnakas	garlic	**šerniena**	boar
daržovės	vegetables	**slyva**	plum
dešrelės	sausage	**špinatai**	spinach
elniena	venison	**steikas**	steak
fazanas	pheasant	**sterkas**	pike perch
grybai	mushrooms	**stirniena**	deer
jautiena	beef	**sultinys**	broth
kalafioras	cauliflower	**sūris**	cheese
keptas	fried	**troškinys**	stew
kiauliena	pork	**tunas**	tuna
kopūstas	cabbage	**ungurys**	eel
krevetės	shrimp	**upėtakis**	trout
kumpis	ham	**veršiena**	veal
lašiša	salmon	**vištiena**	chicken
lietiniai	crepes	**virtas**	boiled
menkė	cod	**vyšnios**	cherry

HANDY TRAVEL TIPS

An A–Z Summary of Practical Information

A

ACCOMMODATION

A great deal of time, effort and money has been recently spent to produce some swish establishments in which the visitor can rest his or her weary head. Most hotels are child-friendly, but not pet-friendly. Rates in Vilnius, as opposed to the coastal regions, tend not to fluctuate seasonally. However, hotel prices can sometimes be lower in winter as hotels scramble to fill up their empty rooms. Breakfast is usually included in the price at smaller and mid-range hotels, but will cost extra at the more upmarket ones.

Most hotels do not have facilities for wheelchair-bound customers, although this is changing as zoning laws make wheelchair access obligatory in new hotels. If you need to find a hotel with disabled facilities, it's best to ask staff pointed and numerous questions about what the hotel has to offer.

It's always best to book your room before entering the country. Many of the newer hotels have online booking systems, making the experience hassle-free. Large hotels are hardly ever booked to capacity, but the cosier bed-and-breakfast or cheaper options can be filled in the summer. If you arrive without a reservation, the Vilnius Tourist Information centre in the railway station can give you listings of accommodation. All hotels are graded by the Lithuanian Tourism Board, but the star system is based on the number of amenities not the level of service.

I'd like a ...	**Aš norėčiau ...**
single room	**vienviečio kambario**
double room	**dviviečio kambario**
with a bath	**su vonia**
with a shower	**su dušu**
What's the rate per day?	**Kiek kainuoja viena diena?**

AIRPORT

The Vilnius International Airport *(Vilnaus oro uostas)* is about 5km (3 miles) south of the city. Although recently renovated, the place hasn't changed much since its construction. Only flights originating in Europe take off and land from here. The major airlines are Lufthansa and SAS, and the smaller companies include Aeroflot, Air Baltic, Lithuanian Airlines (LAL) and Polish Airlines (LOT).

The cheapest way into town is bus No. 1 to the railway station or No. 2, which stops at both Gedimino prospektas and, north of the river, Konstitucijos prospektas. Both buses take about 25 minutes for the trip and cost 1 Lt. They can be picked up outside the arrivals hall. For 1 Lt extra you can take mini-buses No. 15, 21, 23 or 47, all of which stop in the city centre on Gedimino. Bus drivers don't speak English.

The easiest and fastest way into the centre is to get a taxi from the rank outside the arrivals hall. Your trip should cost you no more than 30 Lt under any circumstances, and should usually be between 10 and 15 Lt. The best way to ensure that your ride is what it should be is to call a taxi. The two companies with good reputations and the occasional English-speaking operator are Martono taksi (tel: 240 00 44) and Vilniaus taxi (tel: 212 88 88).

I need a taxi at the airport.	**Aš noriu taksi į oro uostą.**
How much?	**Kiek kainuoja?**
That's too much!	**Per daug! Labai daug!**
Does this bus go to …?	**Ar šitas autobusas važiuoja į ...?**

B

BUDGETING FOR YOUR TRIP

Flying to Vilnius and paying for a hotel will be your largest expenses. Although prices are rising and steadily keeping pace with other EU members, Lithuania still delivers a lot for your money.

Travel to Vilnius. Scheduled flights from London to Vilnius cost any-where from £80 to £600. Prices take a significant dip during the winter months with the exception of the Christmas and New Year holidays. There are no direct flights between the US and Lithuania.

Airport transfer. Public transport costs 1 Lt when the ticket is purchased from the driver. Taxi fares should be less than 30 Lt to any destination near or in the Old Town.

Transport. Your options are the state-owned blue-and-yellow city buses or trolleybuses, where tickets are inexpensive (70–1 Lt). For a bit more (2 Lt), mini-buses provide a cleaner form of transport. However, most destinations are easily reached on foot.

Taxis. Taxi rides within the centre of the city should never be more than 20 Lt, and usually are in the 10–15 Lt range. The easiest way to ensure a safe and uninflated cost is to phone for a taxi or ask hotel reception or restaurant staff to call one for you.

Car hire. Car rental prices hover around 200 Lt per day and usually come with unlimited mileage.

Hotels. Mid-range double rooms per night will cost about 300–400 Lt. In winter prices come down to 250–300 Lt.

Meals and Entertainment. As with most things in life, the nicer your surroundings the more you'll pay. Half pints of beer cost anywhere from 5–13 Lt and are often a few litas cheaper than bottled water. A three-course meal per person without alcohol is 40–90 Lt. Tickets per person to the Philharmonic usually cost about 10–50 Lt.

Museums and Attractions. Admission fees to museums are nominal, usually under 5 Lt. Festivals are usually outdoors and free.

C

CAMPING

Vilnius' typically harsh winters preclude camping from autumn to spring. Lithuanian summers can also be soggy affairs, so it is best to come prepared. Camping in national parks is popular (*for useful website addresses, see page 77–9*).

CAR HIRE (RENTAL)

The Old Town's many pedestrians-only and narrow streets, together with a dearth of parking spots (only the top hotels offer parking), mean that a car in Vilnius is more of a hindrance than a help. Explore on foot, except if you plan to visit sights outside the city, in which case a car is the best way to get around because public transport, although cheap, is often inconvenient. Drive with care; Lithuanians are not the most cautious of drivers.

Most of the major international hire-car companies, including Avis, Budget, Europcar and Hertz, can be found in Vilnius. All have rental desks at the airport, and some also have offices in the city centre. All companies require a valid driver's licence and the driver to be at least 21 years of age.

Prices tend to be lower than in Western Europe and the US. Pricing structures are the same as in most countries with added fees for an additional driver, insurance, mileage and the like. If you plan to take your rental car outside the country, you will need special documents for the border. However, many rental companies have special deals for one-way travel within all three Baltic States.

Avis: at the airport, tel: 232 93 16; fax: 232 93 16; <www.avis.com>.
Budget: at the airport, tel: 230 67 08; fax: 230 67 09; <www.budget.com>.
Hertz: at the airport, tel/fax: 232 93 01; in the city, Kalvarijų 14; tel: 272 69 40; fax: 272 69 70; <www.hertz.com>.

Europcar: at the airport, tel/fax: 216 34 42; in the city, Stuokos-Gucevičiaus 9-1; tel: 212 02 07; fax: 212 04 39; <www.europcar.lt>.
Sixt: at the airport, tel: 239 56 36; fax: 239 56 35; <www.sixt.lt>.

CLIMATE

The only time you can guarantee that it will not be raining in Vil-nius is when it is so cold it can only snow. The is average is 10 days' rain every month, which during the wetter months of January and February is augmented by another 10 days of snow and sleet. These northern and typically harsh winters are off-set by pleasant, albeit short, summers where the hours of sunshine are longer than those of darkness.

The temperature is a median between Moscow and Warsaw. Win-ters can be exceedingly cold and temperatures can dip way below freezing. This, compounded by wind, can make even the most stoic person start to complain. Summers tend to be mild, although an oc-casional heat wave can make Vilnius feel like a swamp. Before au-tumn sets in, the city is usually lucky enough to get a *bobų vasara* (old ladies' summer) which is an extra week of warm temperatures.

	J	F	M	A	M	J	J	A	S	O	N	D
°C	-3.5	-1.7	3	11	18	21	22	22	16	10	4	0.5
	-9	-8	-4	1.6	8	11	12	11	8	3	-0.9	-7
°F	26	29	38	52	65	70	72	70	62	50	38	31
	16	18	25	35	45	51	54	53	50	38	30	23

CLOTHING

Expect some form of precipitation during your stay in Vilnius. A waterproof jacket and shoes will prove indispensable. Most build-ings tend to be overheated in the freezing winter months, so dress-ing in layers is always a good idea. Bring not only a heavy coat but also a hat, gloves and thick winter socks. Even in July and August,

Vilnius can sometimes be quite crisp and cool, especially at night, so a warm sweater or light jacket is advisable. When dining at the city's swisher establishments, smart attire is recommended.

CRIME AND SAFETY

Vilnius is a relatively safe city. Violent crime rates are low. Less serious crimes such as pick-pocketing and car theft are not unheard of, however, and you should exercise caution by not flaunting wads of money or expensive jewellery, and being alert in less travelled areas or places with large numbers of tourists. At night walk in well-lit areas.

Where is the police station?	**Kur policijos nuovada?**
My ... has been stolen. passport/handbag/wallet	**Man pavogė ... pasą/rankinę/piniginę**
Stop thief!	**Stok, vagis!**
Help!	**Gelbėkite!**
Go away!	**Pradink!**

CUSTOMS AND ENTRY REQUIREMENTS

Passports/Visas. EU citizens do not need a visa to travel to Lithuania. Visa-free travel agreements also exist with Australia, Canada, New Zealand, Switzerland, the US and all Nordic countries. Anyone planning to stay longer than 90 days will need to apply for a residency and/or work permit.

Vaccinations. You do not need to get vaccinations unless travelling from an infected area.

Currency Restrictions. If you are taking in more than 10,000 Lt in cash you must declare it. Citizens of Belarus are not allowed to bring in more than 600 Lt in cash.

Customs. A reasonable amount of alcohol, cigarettes, cigars, and perfume are allowed into the country for personal use. As with all EU countries, visitors to Lithuania are prohibited from bringing in meat and dairy products or rooted or planted vegetable products. You can take away as much artwork as you wish but duty of 10–20 percent must be paid on any piece more than 50 years old before going through customs at the airport. Most antiques shops can do the paperwork for you. Otherwise you must make an appointment with the Committee of Cultural Heritage (Šnipiškiu 3, tel: 272 40 05 or 272 41 13). Take your passport and at least two photographs of the artwork in question. They will then charge you the duty and provide all necessary paperwork.

D

DRIVING

Road Conditions. In comparison with the roads of neighbouring Poland, Lithuanian roads are absolutely beyond reproach: most are new or at the very least kept in good working order. The main roads outside Vilnius (A2 towards Riga, and A1 towards Klaipėda) are well maintained. However, when travelling on smaller roads or in rural areas it is not uncommon to come across a horse-drawn wagon or a tractor slowing up traffic.

Rules and Regulations. Drive on the right and overtake on the left. Speed limits are 50–60km/h (31–37mph) in towns and cities, 90km/h (55mph) on country roads, and 100km/h (62mph) on the Vilnius–Kaunas motorway. On all other motorways the speed limits from 1 October to 1 April are 110km/h (68mph) and during the rest of the year 130km/h (80 mph). Although it often seems that no one bothers to observe the speed limits, police with radar guns are stationed along most major thoroughfares. Most drivers opt to pay their fines in cash on the spot to avoid having to go to a police station to do so. Be aware also that even if you are driving through an apparently rural landscape, a town's limits extend up to the point where the sign of the town with a cross through it stands. Police frequently set up speed traps in these non-populated areas where the urban speed limit still applies.

If you have an accident, you are not supposed to move your vehicle until the police have arrived. The use of mobile phones by drivers is prohibited without hands-free equipment. Lithuanian law requires that headlights be kept on at all times, day and night. Drivers are considered under the influence of alcohol and therefore subject to arrest if they have a 0.4 percent alcohol level in their blood. It is best not to drink at all if you are driving.

Fuel Costs. Fuel is sold by the litre. Premium unleaded petrol costs about 2.8 Lt/litre and diesel is about 2.3 Lt/litre. Fuel is sold in 92, 95 and 98 octane and typically will have an E, which stands for unleaded. Diesel pumps are marked with a D. Most petrol stations are open 24 hours except for small ones outside major metropolitan areas. Almost all accept credit cards and are self-service, meaning you put the petrol in yourself and then go inside to pay. Some of the newer stations have machines attached to the pump where you can pay with cash or a credit card.

petrol	**benzino**
Full tank, please.	**Prašau pilną benzino baką.**
My car (automobile) has broken down.	**Sugedo mašina (automobilis).**
There's been an accident.	**Įvyko avarija.**
Can I park here?	**Ar galiu čia statyti mašiną?**

Parking. Parking space is at a premium in the Old Town and city centre. If you do find a spot, you'll have to pay for the privilege during the day up until 8pm. The cost is 2L, payable to a ticket seller on the street. Place the receipt prominently on your dashboard.

If you Need Help. Mototuras (tel: 880 000 000; <www.mototuras.
lt>), a private company operated by the Lithuanian Automobile
Association (LAS), provides emergency road-side assistance.

Bringing Your Own Car to Vilnius. At the border you will be asked
to show a valid driver's licence, vehicle registration and/or ownership
documents, and proof of insurance while in Lithuania (i.e. a Green
Card extending your regular car insurance). All vehicles in Lithuania are required to carry a fluorescent warning triangle, fire extin-
guisher and first-aid kit. You must also have a national identity sticker
on the rear of your vehicle. Breakdown insurance is advisable.

Road Signs. Instructional road signs are for the most part standard
European symbols. Be aware that Gedimino is open to two-way traffic only at certain points during the day, which seem to change on a
fairly regular basis. On motorways, road signs indicating the more
touristy destinations are common, but can be absent for smaller towns.
You'll need a good map if you plan to travel off the beaten track.

No entry	**Įvažiuoti draudžiama**
Caution!	**Atsargiai, dėmesio!**
Pedestrian zone	**Pėsčiųjų zona**
Road work	**Kelio darbai**

E

ELECTRICITY

Standard voltage in Vilnius is 220V/50Hz AC with standard two-pin
European sockets. In some older unrenovated buildings occasionally
one can find the thinner Russian plugs, but this is very uncommon.
Finding converters for US and UK appliances is nearly impossible so
visitors should purchase converters in their home country.

EMBASSIES AND CONSULATES

Australia. Vilniaus 23; tel: 212 33 69; fax: 212 33 69
UK. Antakalnio 2; tel: 246 29 00; fax: 246 29 01.
USA. Akmenų 6; tel: 266 55 00; fax: 266 55 10.
Canada. Gedimino 64; tel: 249 09 50; fax: 249 78 65.

I want to contact my embassy.	**Aš noriu susisiekti su savo ambasada.**

EMERGENCIES

Vilnius has an all-encompassing emergency number, 112. English-speaking personnel are usually on hand, though a non-English speaker may get your call.

Police: 02
Fire: 01
Paramedics: 03

Fire!	**Gaisras!**
Help!	**Gelbėkite!**
Call the police.	**Pakvieskite policiją.**
Please send an ambulance/ police car/fire truck to…	**Atsiųskit greitąją pagalbą/ policiją/gaisrinę į …**

G

GAY AND LESBIAN TRAVELLERS

Homosexuality is legal, but conservative social attitudes mean that openly gay couples are never seen on the city's streets and squares. However, a small male gay scene does exist in Vilnius. Most gay and lesbian organisations exist underground and are often geared towards providing a social/dating scene. For more information, see the following websites: <www.gayline.lt> and <www.gay.lt>.

GENEALOGY

Those wanting to track down information about their Lithuanian ancestry can get help from several specialist agencies:

Lithuanian Central State Archive *(Lietuvos centrinis valstybės archyvas)*. Milašiaus 21; tel: 276 52 90; fax: 276 53 18. A directory of people living in Lithuania during the Nazi occupation (1941–2).
Lithuanian State Historical Archive *(Lietuvos valstybės istorijos archyvas)*. Gerosios Vilties 10; tel: 213 74 82; fax: 213 76 12. Church registry from 1940 to the present.
Vilnius Civilian Archive *(Vilnaus civilinės metrikacijos dokumentų archyvas)*. Kalinausko 21; tel: 233 78 46. Birth, death and marriage certificates from 1940 to the present.

GETTING THERE

By Air. There are no direct flights from North America or Australia to Vilnius. The Lithuanian national carrier, *Lietuvos avialinijos* or LAL, can be found at <www.lal.lt>. Other European carriers are Aeroflot, Air Baltic, Austrian Airlines, Czech Airlines, Estonian Air, Finnair, LOT (Polish national carrier), Lufthansa and SAS. There are also charter flight companies such as Aurela and Aviavilsa.

LAL offers direct flights to and from a number of major European points of departure, including London Gatwick, Paris Charles de Gaulle, Frankfurt, Copenhagen, Stockholm and Warsaw. Connections from the US – many will require at least two stopovers – are possible with American Airlines, Delta Airlines, Continental Airlines, Northwest Airlines and United Airlines. From Australia and New Zealand, use an airline such as Singapore Airlines, Qantas or Air New Zealand which can connect you to Vilnius through its regional hub for onward flights.

By Rail. For long-distance travel, trains can provide a far better level of comfort than road transport, not to mention a greater chance of getting some sleep. Train timetables and other useful information in English can be viewed on the Lithuanian rail website, <www.litrail.lt>. For the most part ticket sales agents at the Vilnius railway station do not speak English so it is best to write down the day, time and destination on a piece of paper and hand it to the agent.

By Road. Travelling by bus can be cheaper and faster than by train to certain destinations, such as Riga. Eurolines, <www.eurolines.com>, service numerous destinations in Europe to Vilnius.

GUIDES AND TOURS

Most hotels have an arrangement with a tour company. Bus tours of the Old Town with commentary in English are also available. In good weather look for the open-top bus parked at the end of Didžioji, otherwise a US-style school bus will be there. The In Via company (tel: 231 00 49; <www.invia.lt>) and Vilnius City Tour (tel: 261 55 58; <www.vilniuscitytour.com>) have tours of the Old Town or Trakai beginning at Cathedral Square. Specialised tours are also offered – check with the tourist office for operators *(see page 126)*. One notable firm is Avanturas (tel: 265 23 55; <www.avanturas.lt>), which has a number of innovative specialised tours of Vilnius and even ecotourism getaways.

H

HEALTH AND MEDICAL CARE

Visiting Lithuania poses no health concerns. However, foreigners needing medical attention will have to pay for all services. Should something occur during your stay it is best to have traveller's insurance and the extra funds with which to pay any medical bills.

Pharmacies can be found by looking for the word *vaistinė* and a green cross, which will usually be illuminated. The only centrally located,

24-hour pharmacy in Vilnius is at Gedimino 27. The range of drugs available in other parts of Europe and the US may not be available here.

There are a few medical facilities that cater for foreigners and often with significantly higher prices than their Lithuanian counterparts. The Baltic American Clinic in the northeastern suburb of Antakalnis (Nemenčinės 54a; tel: 234 20 20; <www.baclinic.com>) is open 24 hours and is by far the most recommended and well known.

Where's the ...?	**Kur yra ...?**
chemist	**vaistinė**
hospital	**ligoninė**
dentist	**dantų gydytojas**
I'm sick.	**Aš sergu.**
Where can I find a doctor who speaks English?	**Kur galiu rasti gydytoją, kas kalba angliškai?**

HITCHHIKING

Hitchhiking is an unsafe method of transport; hitchhikers have been murdered or raped. That said, it is relatively common to see people flagging down cars for a ride outside the city. Often they are young people, mostly students who having moved to the city for their studies are visiting their families at weekends. Women travelling alone should exercise great caution if hitchhiking.

L

LANGUAGE

The Lithuanian language is of Indo-European origin and is one of the two extant Baltic languages (Latvian is the other). It's only other relative is Sanskrit. There are seven cases, five declension patterns and without the stress on the correct syllable an attempt at speaking will remain just that. The language is therefore difficult to command. Luckily, most Vilnius residents are multi-lingual. Many of them speak English, especially in hotels and restaurants in the Old Town and city centre.

There are a few letters uncommon to Western European languages. The consonants with hacheks are č which is a 'ch' sound, š which is a 'sh' sound, and ž which is a 'zh' sound. The vowels are į which is long i (as in meet), ė which is between an i and e, ų which is a 'yu' sound (as in root), and ū which is a more guttural version of the 'yu' sound.

Do you speak English?	**Ar jus kalbate angliškai?**
I don't speak Lithuanian.	**Aš nekalbu lietuviškai.**
Good morning/Good afternoon	**Labas rytas/Laba diena**
Good evening	**Labas vakaras**
Good night	**Labanakt**
Goodbye	**Viso gero**
See you later	**Iki pasimatymo**
Nice to meet you	**Labai malonu**
Please/thank you	**Prašau/ačiū**
Excuse me (sorry)	**Atsiprašau**
It's (everything's) ok	**Viskas gerai**
Yes/No	**Taip/Ne**

LAUNDRY AND DRY CLEANING

Many of the more expensive hotels will take care of your dry cleaning and washing – for a price. In the centre, a reputable dry-cleaning company is Jogl at Jasinskio 16.

M

MAPS

Maps of the city centre and Old Town are available at both of the city's Tourist Information Offices *(see page 126)*, although most hotels carry maps. Most magazine city guides contain decent maps. Many of these publications can be found at your hotel reception desk for free or for a nominal fee. The most detailed maps of the city and surrounding area are produced by Jana Seta and can be found in many of the city's bookshops. Road maps can be bought at most petrol stations.

MEDIA

Television. Most major hotels will have rooms with satellite televisions; however, the majority of them will come only with the basics of BBC World, CNN and SkyNews. Foreign-language programmes on regular Lithuanian channels will always be dubbed into Lithuanian. At least one station will be available in Russian and another in Polish.

Radio. The BBC World Service can be heard daily on 95.5FM. Lietuvos radijas, <www.lrt.lt>, carries local news in English, beginning at 9pm every day, on 102.6FM. Voice of America, <www.voa.com>, can also be found on short-wave radio.

Press. The weekly English-language newspaper, *The Baltic Times*, covers all three Baltic capitals and their surroundings. For business news, try the monthly *Lithuanian Business Review* magazine, carried by larger bookshops. The Tallinn-based *City Paper* magazine has news, listings and editorials covering all three Baltic capitals. Lastly, the magazine *Vilnius In Your Pocket*, <www.inyourpocket.com>, carries listings and editorials on the city and country.

MONEY

The unit of currency in Lithuania is the *litas* (Lt), which comes in - denominations of 1, 10, 20, 50, 100, 200 and 500 Lt notes. The 1Lt banknote, emblazoned with the not-so-cheery face of Julija Beniuševičiūtė-Žymantienė, is fast disappearing from circulation so they make for good and inexpensive mementos of your visit. The coins can be divided into the valuable – 1, 2 and 5 Lt – and the nearly worthless centai variety, of which there are 50, 20, 10, 5, 2 and 1. The *litas* is pegged to the euro at a stable rate of 3.45.

Currency Exchange. Exchange bureaux, inside hotels and banks, are open between 9am and 5pm. Currency exchange outside those times can be difficult. Most banks and exchange bureaux charge a nominal percentage commission. Make sure to have your passport handy, especially when exchanging currency in banks.

Credit Cards. Almost all upmarket or mid-range establishments such as hotels, restaurants, nightclubs, bars and shops, will accept most major credit cards. To be on the safe side, always check before making your purchase.

ATMs. There are ATMs every few metres in the Old Town and city centre. This is one of the easiest ways to 'carry' money. In the countryside, however, cash is king, so take enough with you when travelling outside Vilnius. Cards will be accepted as long as they are tied to the Cirrus or Visa network.

Traveller's Cheques. Perhaps the safest way to carry large amounts of cash, traveller's cheques provide security in the case of loss or theft. Banks and exchange bureaux will exchange them for you, but they cannot be used as currency.

OPENING HOURS

Banks are usually open from 9am to 5pm or sometimes an hour later. Shops open around 10am and can close any time between 6pm to 8pm. Shops in the centre and Old Town will usually have longer hours.

Bars and restaurants stay open until 11pm, if not later during the week, and those geared to a drinking crowd will remain open until 4am at weekends. Finding something to eat late in the evening in the Old Town or centre is usually unproblematic as long as you aren't too picky.

Museums and galleries are usually open 10am–5pm and are closed one day a week, usually a Monday or Sunday.

The kiosks littering the city streets sell the basics – water, soft drinks, cigarettes and magazines. They are usually open very late if not around the clock.

P

POLICE

Police *(policija)* patrol the Old Town and city centre on foot in pairs. Traffic police *(kelių policija)* wear an almost identical green uniform. Routine traffic stops and speed traps are common. Fines are usually paid in cash on the spot, otherwise the driver will have to queue at either a bank (usually for parking tickets) or a police station (for moving violations) and then pay the fine. Most people choose to pay the amount stated by the officer in order to save themselves the extra time and inconvenience.

Where's the police station?	**Kur policijos nuovada?**
I've lost my...	**Pamečiau ... savo.**
passport/luggage	**pasą/bagažą**
I'm lost.	**Aš esu paklydęs (paklydusi).**

POST OFFICES

The postal system is reliable and inexpensive. The main post office in Vilnius is at Gedimino 7 (open Mon–Fri 7am–7pm, Sat 9am–4pm; closed Sun). There is also a major post office in the Old

Town at Vokiečių 7 (open Mon–Fri 8am–7pm, Sat 8am–3pm; closed Sun). Postal rates for international letters start at about 3 Lt.

I want to send this by ...	**Aš norėčiau išsiusti tai...**
airmail	**oro paštu**
express	**skubiu persiuntimu**

PUBLIC HOLIDAYS

Government offices and banks close for the following holidays:

1 January	New Year's Day	**Naujieji Metai**
16 February	Independence Day	**Nepriklausomybės diena**
11 March	Restoration of Independence Day	**Nepriklausomybės atkūrimo diena**
1 May	Day of the Workers	**Darbo diena**
24 June	St John's Day (Midsummer)	**Joninės**
6 July	Lithuanian Statehood Day (Crowning of Mindaugas)	**Lietuvos valstybės diena (Mindaugo karūnavimo)**
15 August	Feast of the Assumption	**Žolinė**
1 November	All Saints' Day	**Vėlinės**
25–6 December	Christmas	**Šv Kalėdos**

All major Christian holidays on the Gregorian calendar tend to be city-wide holidays with the two most important being Easter *(Velykos)* weekend and the Assumption of the Virgin. The first Sunday in May is Mother's Day when most shops close for the day, although restaurants and bars stay open, some with shorter working hours. Several holidays are commemorated without everyone taking a day off work and Lithuanian flags are hung outside homes. These include Defenders of Freedom

(13 January), Day of Mourning and Hope (14 June), Black Ribbon Day (marking the Molotov-Ribbentrop signing on 23 August), Crowning of Vytautas the Great (8 September) and Constitution Day (25 October).

PUBLIC TRANSPORT

Using public transport will not be the most pleasant part of a stay in Vilnius. Trolleybuses and buses are old and smelly. Also, most systems operate from 5:30am to 11pm, so late-night travel is by foot or taxi. Public transport is, however, inexpensive and covers most of the city, excluding the Old Town.

City Buses. The blue-and-yellow buses are state-owned. Tickets for them can be purchased at a *Lietuva spauda* kiosk or on board the bus. Once on the bus you must validate your ticket in one of the boxes provided. Failure to do so will result in a fine by a ticket inspector. Private bus company tickets can only be bought on buses.

Trolleybuses. Riding a trolleybus in Vilnius is the easiest way to travel back in time to the Soviet era. As on the city's buses, tickets can be purchased on board or from *Lietuva spauda* kiosks, but must be validated on board.

Microbuses. This is the newest and cleanest form of transport through the city. Microbus routes are subject to change as they are privately owned and operated. Most have signs in their front windows giving a general idea of their trajectory. To get on one, just flag it down, get in, sit down and tell the driver where you would like to be dropped off. Since no one will usually speak English it is best to have decent Lithuanian pronunciation skills or have your destination written down.

Long-distance Buses. Buses are more popular than trains for most domestic destinations. The bus station is at Sodų 22, <www.toks.lt>, across from the railway station.

Trains. Tickets can be purchased at the station which is located at Geležinkelio 16 (see <www.litrail.lt> for information). On overnight trains there are three classes of ticket. The cheapest is *obschii*, which is a sitting place only. *Platzkart* is a bed in a four-person room and *coupe* is a softer bed in a four-person compartment with a door that locks. Women travelling alone should be aware that it is not uncommon for them to end up in a coupe with three men overnight, although a word in the ear of the train compartment manager once on board can sometimes get the sleeping arrangements changed.

Taxis. Generally, taxi drivers will not take advantage of vigilant oreigners. Most horror stories of inflated taxi prices occur when foreigners are inebriated or when the meter clicks away at a superfast rate and goes unnoticed. To avoid being ripped off, pay attention to your surroundings. It's cheaper to phone for a taxi instead of hailing one off the street. Two reputable firms that occasionally have English-speakers on staff are Martono taksi (tel: 240 00 44) and Vilniaus taksi (tel: 212 88 88).

How much is the fare to …?	**Kiek kainuoja bilietas ...?**
I want a ticket to ...	**Aš norėčiau bilieto į ...**
single (one way)	**į vieną pusę**
return (roundtrip)	**bilieto į abi puses**
first/second class	**pirma/antra klasė**
When is the ... train to ...?	**Kada išvažiuoja ... traukinys į ...?**
first/next/last	** pirmasis/sekantis/paskutinis**
How long does the journey take?	**Ar ilga kelionė?**
Will you tell me when to get off?	**Prašau man pasakyti kur išlipti?**
Take me to this address.	**Nuvežkite mane šiuo adresu.**
Please stop here.	**Prašau čia sustoti.**

R

RELIGION

The country for the most part is Catholic, but smaller groups, notably Russian Orthodox, also exist. English-language services are held at the Evangelical-Lutheran church on Vokiečių 20, <www.icvilnius. org>. Other churches have erratically scheduled English-langauge services; look outside their doors for notices.

T

TELEPHONES

Public telephones *(taksofonas)* are sprinkled throughout the city and all except for a few archaic coin-operated ones require pre-paid telephone cards *(telefono kortelė)* that can be purchased at *Lietuvos spauda* kiosks and post offices.

The international code for Lithuania is 370, the city code for Vilnius is 5. When calling a Vilnius number from the city itself just dial the seven-digit number. When calling Vilnius from outside the city you must first dial 8, wait for the changed tone, then 5 and the number. Lithuanian mobile phone numbers always begin with an 8. When calling a Lithuanian mobile from abroad drop the 8 so that the number begins with 6.

Hotels often charge exorbitant rates for international and sometimes even local calls, so check with the front desk before using your room's telephone. Although public telephones can be used for international calls, their partially sheltered and central location can make intimate conversations difficult. For those staying for longer than a few days the purchase of a pre-paid SIM card for a mobile phone is a good idea. Bitė (Gedimino 39; <www.bite.lt>), Omnitel (Gedimino 12; <www. omnitel.lt>) and TELE2 (Vienuolio 12; <www.tele2.lt>) all provide such services.

To call abroad, dial 00 then the country code: Australia 61, Canada and the US 1, Ireland 353, New Zealand 64, UK 44.

TICKETS

There is a central ticket office (tel: 212 11 81; <www.bilietai.lt>) on the square at Gedimino 9a. It is almost always cheaper to buy tickets directly from the box office rather than through a travel agency. To get a list of current shows pick up a brochure from Vilnius Tourist Information.

TIME ZONES

Lithuania is in the Eastern European Time Zone (GMT+2hrs). Summer time or daylight saving is observed (GMT+3hrs). The following chart shows the time in various cities in summer.

San Francisco	New York	London	**Vilnius**	Sydney
2am	5am	10am	**noon**	7pm

TIPPING

In restaurants and bars with table service simply rounding up the bill is considered sufficient, certainly nothing more than 5 percent for lunch and perhaps 10 percent for dinner. Porters should be tipped a few *litas*.

TOILETS

Public toilets are few and far between. Your best bet is to duck into a bar or restaurant, in which case you should also pay for a cup of coffee. It's a good idea to carry your own tissue or toilet paper as even the cleanest facilities can run out of toilet paper.

Where are the toilets?	**Kur tualetai?**

TOURIST INFORMATION

The best source of information before leaving for Lithuania is the internet. However, there are a few private companies that specialise in travel to Lithuania. Two of the largest in the UK are Regent

Holidays (tel: 0117 921 1711; fax: 0117 925 4866; <www.regent-holidays.co.uk>) and Baltic Holidays (tel: 0870 757 9233; fax: 0870 120 2973; <www.balticholidays.com>).

Vilnius has three Tourist Information centres. The one at the train station and the other at Vilniaus 22 have the same working hours (open Mon–Fri 9am–6pm, Sat–Sun 10am–4pm). The third one is inside the Town Hall at Didžioji 31 (open Mon–Fri 10am–6pm; closed Sat–Sun).

W

WEBSITES

The following websites may help you plan your trip.
<www.vilnius.lt>
<www.turizmas.vilnius.lt>
Internet cafés. Find coffee and computers at the following:
Bazė. Gedimino 50/2; tel: 249 77 01. Open 24hrs.
Collegium. Pilies 2; tel: (8-698) 201 18. Open daily 8am–12pm.

Y

YOUTH HOSTELS

A bed in a communal room costs around 30 Lt. The hostels below are not far from the centre. Be sure to ask about curfews.

Arts Academy Hostel. Latako 2; tel: 212 01 76; fax: 210 54 44. Expect to pay for sheets. Check-out time is 10am. Parking available.
IYH Filaretai. Filaretų 17; tel: 215 46 27; fax: 212 01 49; <www.filaretaihostel.lt>. Clean and comfortable surroundings in Užupis.
Old Town Hostel. Aušros Vartų 20-10; tel: 262 53 57; fax: 268 59 67. Right in the heart of the Old Town.
Vilniaus Jaunųjų Turistų centras (Vilnius Youth Tourist Centre). Polocko 7; tel: 261 35 76; fax: 262 77 42. Located in Užupis. The 16 rooms are all triples or quads. A bit dilapidated, but charming.

Recommended Hotels

Many new hotels have sprung up in the Old Town and city centre alongside renovated ones, giving travellers a wide range of accommodation options. Although large hotels are rarely booked solid, it is always best to make accommodation reservations before arriving in Vilnius. Budget hotels and bed-and-breakfast establishments are more likely to be booked out, especially during the summer months and around the Christmas and New Year holidays. Rates are based on the cost of a double room per night. Some of the larger hotels tend to give pricing in euros. Breakfast is sometimes not included, and usually costs an extra 40 Lt per day. Most of the newly built hotels offer some facilities for disabled travellers. Contact hotels directly for information about their facilities.

The following hotels cover most areas of town, but are predominantly in the Old Town and city centre, and range from small, independently owned places to large hotels managed by international corporations.

If calling from outside Lithuania, dial 00 370 5 before the numbers listed in this guide.

€€€€€	500–700 Lt
€€€€	400–500 Lt
€€€	300–400 Lt
€€	200–300 Lt
€	Under 200 Lt

OLD TOWN

Apia Guest House €€ *Šv Ignoto 12; tel: 212 34 26; fax: 212 36 18; <www.apia.lt>*. The price is reasonable, the location next to the university is wonderful and the rooms and public areas are clean. Taken together, these factors make this place a more interesting proposition than it would be in another city, given the few facilities on offer. Rooms have telephones and satellite TVs. A nice touch is breakfast served in your room. Parking.

Atrium €€€ *Pilies 10; tel: 210 77 77; fax: 210 77 70; <www. atrium.lt>.* What are quite possibly the largest rooms in Vilnius can be found in this hotel on a bustling pedestrian street. The dark-blue leather couches, cordless phones, in-room safes and king-sized beds add to the luxurious feel. The high ceilings and large spaces make this a good option for those travelling in a large nonbudget-conscious group who plan on hosting in-room cocktail parties. Restaurant. Sauna. Most major credit cards accepted.

Barbacan Palace €€€ *Bokšto 19; tel: 266 08 40; fax: 266 08 41; <www.barbacan.lt>.* Patriotic artworks adorn most of the beige and green rooms in this comfortable hotel located down the road from the Artillery Bastion. All come complete with satellite TVs, heated bathroom floors and baths. Other perks include in-room internet access, parking and basement bowling lanes. Apartments are also available. Most major credit cards accepted.

Bernadinų Guest House € *Bernadinų 5; tel: 261 51 34; fax: 260 84 21.* Located on a winding Old Town street, this diminutive but comfortable guesthouse offers small, cosy rooms perfect for the budget traveller. Newly painted walls and duvets from the 1970s create a clean yet retro look. Parking. Most major credit cards accepted.

Centro Kubas €€€ *Stiklių 3; tel: 266 08 60; fax: 266 08 63; <www.centrokubas.lt>.* A small but adorable place with only 14 rooms, this hotel is decorated with restored antique Lithuanian furnishings and domestic paraphernalia. The hotel also has all the modern conveniences such as mini-bars, satellite TVs, free in-room internet access and heated bathroom floors. One room is designed specifically for wheelchair-bound guests. Most major credit cards accepted.

Domus Maria €–€€ *Aušros Vartų 12; tel: 264 48 80; fax: 264 48 78; <domusmaria.vilnesis.lt>.* The rooms at this hotel tucked into a courtyard alongside the Gates of Dawn are renovated monastery cells. Naturally the rooms are a bit small, but the light-wood furniture, high ceilings, large double-paned windows and minimalist lines add to the appeal. Breakfast included. Parking. Most major credit cards accepted.

Eldorado Bed & Breakfast € *tel: (8-686) 838 89; <www.apartamentai.lt>.* Ten apartments are available for short-term or long-term stays. All are located in the Old Town or the city centre and come complete with kitchens and satellite TV.

Europa Imperial Vilnius €€€€ *Aušros Vartų 6; tel: 266 07 70; fax 261 20 00; <www.hoteleuropa.lt>.* The Europa manages to maintain a quiet dignity that belies its location on one of the most highly tourist-travelled streets in the city. All rooms are decorated in a modern albeit generic hotel style, but the numerous amenities, excellent location and light-filled rooms give the place a hard-to-beat individuality. Some rooms have balconies right over Aušros Vartų, while others have views over the Old Town. Breakfast included. Restaurant. Parking and conference facilities. Most major credit cards accepted.

Grotthuss €€€€–€€€€€ *Ligoninės 7; tel: 266 03 22; fax: 266 02 23; <www.grotthushotel.com>.* This charming and cosy hotel in a quiet Old Town location has tastefully decorated and spacious rooms. All rooms come with fluffy feather duvets and baths, and some look out on to the hotel's garden. Breakfast included. Restaurant. Parking and conference facilities. Most major credit cards accepted.

Latako Guest House €€ *Latako 1–2; tel: 261 63 64; <www.latako.ten.lt>.* From the staircase the building may look a bit dilapidated, but the five apartments inside are all renovated and quite large. The furnishings are functional. Telephones, satellite TVs and complete kitchens make these apartments a good base.

Litinterp € *Bernadinų 7–2; tel: 212 38 50; fax: 212 35 59; <www.litinterp.lt>.* As one of the longest-standing guesthouses in the city, Litinterp has survived due to its range of accommodation, reasonable pricing and helpful staff. Some of the rooms are inside family homes while others are fully functional apartments.

Radisson SAS Astorija €€€€€ *Didžioji 35/2; tel: 212 01 10; fax: 212 17 62; <www.radissonsas.com>.* With more than 120 rooms, the Radisson is one of the largest hotels in town. Geared towards an international business clientele, it provides all the usual comforts, including room safes, modem points and mini-bars. Restaurant. Major credit cards accepted.

Relais & Chateaux Stikliai €€€€€ *Gaono 7; tel: 264 95 95; fax: 212 38 70; <www.stikliaihotel.lt>.* This is one of the most luxurious hotels in the city, popular with captains of industry and foreign dignitaries. The rooms are large and the decor is exceptionally stylish and soothing. The attentive staff make certain that guests have trouble-free stays. Apartment rentals are also available in the building. Restaurant, sauna and swimming pool. Most major credit cards accepted.

Rūdninkū Vartai €€ *Rūdninkų 15/46; tel: 261 39 16; fax: 212 05 07.* Vary basic, but clean accommodation on one edge of a quiet street in the Old Town. The decor hasn't been updated since Soviet times, but the staff has a friendly service-oriented attitude. Room amenities, perks or any sort of extras are non-existent.

Shakespeare Boutique Hotel €€€€–€€€€€ *Bernardinų 8/8; tel: 266 58 85; fax: 266 58 86; <www.shakespeare.lt>.* The first true boutique hotel in town is dedicated to the great English playwright. In fact, each of the rooms is named after a famous writer and has decor to match. The staff are particularly attentive. Some rooms only have showers, but all come equipped with VCRs should you want to settle in and watch a film. Restaurant. Most major credit cards accepted.

Shakespeare Too €€€€–€€€€€ *Pilies 34; tel: 266 16 26; fax: 266 16 27; <www.shakespeare.lt>.* Under the same management as the Shakespeare, this hotel is dedicated to great painters, with each room decorated with reproductions of famous works. The most remarked-upon room is the Nude Room with pictures of famous lightly dressed women and a great balcony for people-watching. Most major credit cards accepted.

CITY CENTRE

Ambassador €€ *Gedimino 12; tel: 261 54 50; fax: 212 17 16; <www.ambassador.lt>*. Although the rooms here have been updated since Soviet times, a mentality that furnishings should be utilitarian and not eye-catching seems to have lingered. However, some of the rooms have a view on to the bustling street below and all have TV and telephone.

City Gate €€€ *Bazilijonų 3; tel: 210 73 06; fax: 210 73 07; <www.citygate.lt>*. This appropriately named hotel is just steps from the city wall and the Gates of Dawn. Expect floral curtains and somewhat cramped quarters (unless you opt for the business-class rooms) in this small but cheery and well-located hotel. Breakfast included. Most major credit cards accepted.

City Park €€€€–€€€€€ *Stuokos-Gucevičiaus 3; tel: 212 35 15; fax: 210 74 60; <www.citypark.lt>*. Great location opposite the cathedral. As one of the few truly wheelchair-accessible hotels in the city, this thoroughly modern and spacious hotel caters for all manner of travellers. The smallest details are seen to, so expect a sweet on your pillow each night and free in-room internet access, as well as a mini-bar and satellite TV. Breakfast not included. Most major credit cards accepted.

Conti €€€€ *Raugyklos 7/2; tel: 251 41 11; fax: 251 41 00; <www.contihotel.lt>*. This new and luxurious addition to the Vilnius hotel scene offers soothing and surprisingly spacious rooms swathed in various beige-based colours. The double-paned windows help to ensure a restful night's sleep despite the proximity to the traffic on Pylimo. The staff are very professional. Room amenities include a mini-bar and satellite TV. Secure parking. Restaurant. On-site sauna, gym and conference facilities. Most major credit cards accepted.

Crowne Plaza Vilnius €€€ *Čiurlionio 84; tel: 274 34 00; fax: 274 34 11; <www.cpvilnius. com>.* Opened in 2003, this has all the amenities one would expect from a large, modern hotel: in-room dataports, mini-bars, safes, 24-hour room service. Apart from the stylish interior, the great attraction for most people who stay here is the proximity to Vingis Park. There's a great view from the hotel's 16th-floor bar. Most major credit cards accepted.

Dvaras Manor House €€€ *Tilto 3; tel: 210 73 70; fax: 261 87 83; <www.dvaras.lt>.* With only eight rooms, this diminutive hotel near the cathedral has an intimate, home-like appeal. Rooms come with TV and telephone and are furnished with a variety of Lithuanian knick-knacks. Parking available. Most major credit cards accepted.

Ecotel Vilnius € *Slucko 8; tel: 210 27 00; fax: 210 27 07; <www. ecotel.lt>.* Located over the Green Bridge (Žaliasis tiltas) across the Neris from Gedimino, this modern economy-class hotel is just a 10-minute walk from the Old Town. Its comfortable rooms are popular with business people, groups and those needing large conference facilities. Most major credit cards accepted.

E-Guest House € *Ševčenkos 16; tel: 266 07 30; fax: 233 57 10; <www.e-guesthouse.lt>.* A bit off the beaten path and yet not far from the city centre, this is a comfortable, good-value budget choice. It is also by far one of the most child-friendly options in the city – children under 12 stay free. Adults can amuse themselves by renting a laptop and using their free in-room internet connection. Rooms also come with satellite TV, mini-bar and phone. Parking. Most major credit cards accepted.

Europa City €€ *Jasinskio 14; tel: 251 44 77; fax: 251 44 76; <www.hoteleuropa.lt>.* Located on a street running parallel to the end of Gedimino before it crosses the Neris, Europa City sits in a relatively central location. A large, business-class hotel, it offers satellite TV, mini-bars, safes and dataports in all rooms. The rooms swathed in muted colours make the decor match the ambiance. Parking. Fitness centre. Pool. Most major credit cards accepted.

Mabre Residence €€€€–€€€€€ *Maironio 13; tel: 212 20 87; fax: 212 22 40; <www.mabre.lt>.* Situated around a courtyard right off the edge of the Old Town, this former Orthodox monastery provides pleasant and insular surroundings. The hotel caters mostly for the business traveller, and the staff are suitably efficient. Breakfast is not included. Restaurant. Sauna. Parking. Most major credit cards accepted.

Novotel €€€ *Gedimino 16; tel: 266 62 00; fax: 266 62 01; <www.novotel.com>.* This business-class hotel stands right on one of the city's main thoroughfares. The rooms are spacious, classy and accented by interesting works of art. All the amenities one would expect are present (mini-bars, satellite TV, fitness and business centres) along with wheelchair accessibility. Most major credit cards accepted.

Reval Hotel Lietuva €€€€ *Konstitucijos 20; tel: 272 62 00; fax: 272 62 10; <www.revalhotels.com>.* With almost 300 rooms, a fabulous 22nd-floor bar, restaurant, casino and sauna, this brand new hotel is a virtual city unto itself. For some this will make up for its location on the north side of the Neris (although the Old Town is relatively close). The rooms are not as spacious as one might anticipate, but all are decorated in classic dark colours. Ask for a room with a view of the Old Town. There is one entire floor of non-smoking rooms and the Executive-class rooms all have balconies. Gedimino is a few minutes' walk across the pedestrian White Bridge (Baltasis tiltas).

Rinno €€–€€€ *Vingrių 25; tel: 262 28 28; fax: 262 59 29; <www.rinno.lt>.* Standard-sized rooms with exceptionally large bathrooms can be found at this reasonably priced hotel. All the carpets have the hotel insignia in case you lose track of where you are. Next door to a strip club. Breakfast included. Most major credit cards accepted.

Scandic Neringa Vilnius €€€–€€€€€ *Gedimino 23; tel: 268 19 10; fax: 261 41 60; <www.scandic-hotels.com>.* This Soviet-era hotel on Gedimino has been completely renovated by the

Scandic hotel chain, resulting in a red, blue and wooded decor, with large windows. The rooms are clean and comfortable. Sauna, restaurant, conference and parking facilities. Most major credit cards accepted.

Senatoriai €€ *Tilto 2a; tel: 212 70 56; fax: 212 63 72*. This small hotel is in an excellent location in a back street near the cathedral. Lots of dark wood seems to diminish the already small, if cosy, rooms. Parking available. Most major credit cards accepted.

Telecom Guest House €€ *Vivulskio 13a; tel: 264 48 61; fax: 264 48 60; <www.telecomguesthouse.lt>*. A clean and comfortable hotel decorated by someone enamoured with the colour blue. Although not right in the centre of the action, the hotel makes up for it with a quieter ambiance and a truly helpful and knowledgeable staff. The hotel is in a courtyard up the small hill west of the Old Town off the large thoroughfare of Basanavičiaus Street.

FURTHER AFIELD

Grožio Sala €€ *Sugiharos 3; tel: 230 57 10; fax: 270 57 78; <www.sugihara.lt>*. Grožio Sala (Beauty Island) is for those who want to combine discovering a new city with enjoying a spa holiday. The full-service spa tends to attract many foreign clients and locals wanting a weekend break. The rooms are a few notches above basic. Located within the city limits, the hotel is in the northwest area of Viršuliškės. Most major credit cards accepted.

Le Méridien Villon Resort €€€€ *A-2 motorway; tel: 273 97 00; fax: 265 13 85; <www.lemeridien.com>*. Located 19km (12 miles) north of the city, this out-of-the-way combination spa and hotel offers respite from the exertions of both the workaday world and the tourist trail. Although only a few minutes' drive from the city (the hotel also has shuttle buses to and from the centre), you'll feel as if you are much farther away. A full range of treatments are offered, everything from full body and underwater massage to hydrotherapy and aromatherapy. Most rooms overlook the nearby lake or forest.

Recommended Restaurants

Lithuanian restaurant service can be a little on the laid-back side (or possibly lacking in any sort of attention). Sometimes the waiting staff will make no effort to show their disdain for having been bothered to get your food. At the more inexpensive establishments expect to be charged for everything including condiments. More upmarket places may add a service charge (usually 15 percent) to your bill. Prices listed in this guide are for a typical three-course meal without drinks. Most restaurants serve food throughout the day, but become more crowded during lunch (11am–2pm) and dinner (6–10pm). Credit cards are accepted in most mid- to upper-range establishments, but it is always best to check beforehand.

Once unnecessary in all but the posh places, reservations are becoming more common, though only in upmarket and mid-range restaurants. A telephone call just a few days, rather than weeks, in advance is usually sufficient to procure a table. If calling from outside Lithuania, dial 00 370 5 before the numbers listed in this guide.

€€€€€	Over 75 Lt
€€€€	60–75 Lt
€€€	45–60 Lt
€€	30–45 Lt
€	Under 30 Lt

OLD TOWN

Aqua €€ *Didžioji 28; tel: 260 88 70.* Although not slated to win any design awards, Aqua is nearly always packed due to its inexpensive menu and excellent location. It's a buffet by day, so grab a tray, wait in the queue and point to whichever Lithuanian dish looks good. By night, it's a restaurant – expect prompt and attentive table service. Open Mon–Thur 7.30am–midnight, Fri 7.30am–2am, Sat 10am–2am, Sun 10am–midnight. Major credit cards accepted.

Baltasis Štralis €€€€ *Pilies 26; tel: 231 44 82.* The decor bounces between a generic hotel restaurant and the heyday of Lithuania opulence; however, the food is decidedly and deliciously Lithuanian. The food transcends the mundane variations on meat and potatoes of many other restaurants by the skilful use of spices and herbs. Budget travellers who want to try Lithuanian food should head for the front of the restaurant, which is considered a café and has a cheaper menu than the restaurant. The pancakes, which are large and come with a choice of sauces, are an economical and filling option. Open daily 10am–midnight. Most major credit cards accepted.

Balti Drambliai € *Vilniaus 41; tel: 262 08 75.* Balti Drambliai (White Elephants) is not only the sole vegetarian restaurant in town, it is also completely non-smoking. This is a great place for vegetarians to tuck into a variety of dishes that go beyond the variations on over-boiled cabbage and potato they are often presented with. The waiting staff tend to be lethargic, so come here only if you're in the mood for a leisurely meal. Open Mon–Fri 11am–midnight, Sat–Sun noon–midnight. Most major credit cards accepted.

Čili Kaimas €€ *Vokiečių 8; tel: 231 25 36.* Chickens behind glass windows and fish swimming in a pool create a back-to-basics feel at this family restaurant, one of the better places to sample national dishes. Portions are generous. The large, seemingly labyrinthine premises on two floors can be packed at the weekends and queuing is not unusual. Open Mon–Thur, Sun 10am–midnight, Fri–Sat 10am–4am. Most major credit cards accepted.

El Gaucho Sauno €€€€ *Pilies 10; tel: 210 77 73.* As the only Argentinian steakhouse in Vilnius, the Gaucho manages to impress. Through a courtyard and inside the Atrium Hotel, the restaurant cannot be missed once the cowhide decor is spotted. The food luckily steers clear of any mediocrity with what some consider the best steaks in the city. The portions are large, so come with an appetite. Open daily noon–2am. Most major credit cards accepted.

Freskos €€€ *Didžioji 31; tel: 261 81 33; <www.freskos.lt>.* Located on the back and side of the Town Hall is this paean to theatre. Costumes and posters adorn the walls and sturdy dark wood furnishings create a pleasant ambiance. The international-style food is delicious. Long waits for tables are not uncommon. Open daily 11am–midnight. Most major credit cards accepted.

Gabi €€ *Šv Mykolo 6; tel: 212 36 43.* This original, completely non-smoking restaurant in Vilnius is almost always packed with foreign visitors seeking respite from the cigarette-smoke of the city's other eateries. The food is basic Lithuanian, so expect variations on the meat, potato and cabbage themes. Their 'no photography inside the restaurant' rule, although seemingly archaic, should be adhered to. Open daily 11am–10pm. Most major credit cards accepted.

G-Lounge €€€ *Didžioji 11; tel: 260 94 30; <www.glounge.lt>.* Although this restaurant touts its 'fusion' food as being on par with what one would find in most cosmopolitan cities, it feels more like a goal than the reality. The food is, however, more innovative than in other establishments – expect mostly meat dishes with an Asian twist. Portions tend to be on the small side. Open daily 11.30am–midnight. Most major credit cards accepted.

Lokys €€€ *Stiklių 8; tel: 262 90 46; <www.lokys.lt>.* The city's only restaurant serving game dishes can be found in a courtyard past a wooden bear sculpture. The cellar interior provides the perfect ambiance for trying a wild boar cutlet *(šernienos kepsnys)* or beaver meat stew *(valstietiškas bebrienos troškinys)*. There are a few vegetarian and non-game dishes for those wanting something a bit tamer. Staff are helpful in choosing your courses. The staircase is tiny and diners should exercise caution when coming and going. Open daily noon–midnight. Most major credit cards accepted.

Markus ir Ko €€€€ *Antokolskio 11; tel: 262 31 85.* As one of the oldest steakhouses in the city, Markus ir Ko has managed to keep its customers happy by not changing its winning formula. It serves high-quality beef and everything is *à la carte.* Customers choose their sauce, the cut of beef and side dishes. Located on a small street off of Stiklių. Open daily noon–midnight. Most major credit cards accepted.

La Provence €€€€€ *Vokiečių 22; tel: 261 65 73; <www. laprovence.lt>.* Sumptuous French food right on a main street in the Old Town. This is one of the few places where you can have a dining experience rather than just a plate of food set in front of you. The menu hits on most major influences on French cuisine, including an attractive Provençal fish stew, richly dressed meats and tasty desserts. The space is a lavishly decorated cellar. Open daily 11am–midnight. Most major credit cards accepted.

The Pub €€€ *Dominikonų 9; tel: 261 83 93; <www.pub.lt>.* A British ex-pat spot since it first opened, the Pub is now also a student hangout. The menu has something to satisfy everyone, with salads, pasta dishes, sandwiches and burgers. The food is simple, the staff are impeccably nice and the courtyard area is often home to live entertainment at the weekends. Open Mon–Thur, Sun 11am–2am, Fri–Sat 11am–5am. Most major credit cards accepted.

Savas Kampas €€–€€€ *Vokiečių 4; tel: 212 32 03.* It's hard not to like this earthy little spot. A selection of soups take a while to prepare, but they are definitely worth the wait. The staff never seem to be in too much of a hurry, so lengthy waits are anyway common. Long bench seating in the front room is good for groups while the downstairs cellar is better for those wanting dimmer surroundings. At night the place turns into more of a bar with food rather than a restaurant. There's outdoor seating in summer. Open Mon–Wed 9am–1am, Thur–Fri 9am–3am, Sat 10am–3am, Sun 10am–1am. Most major credit cards accepted.

Skonis ir Kvapas €€ *Trakų 8; tel: 212 28 03.* This teashop-cum-restaurant is tucked into a courtyard of the Old Town. The straightforward food seasoned with fresh herbs makes for a decidedly tasty meal; try the boiled chicken with tarragon. A great selection of teas and coffees rounds off the experience. The two non-smoking back rooms are less crowded. Open Mon–Fri, Sun 8.30am–11pm, Sat 9.30am–11pm. Most major credit cards accepted.

Sonnets €€€€ *Bernadinų 8/8; tel: 266 58 85; <www.shake-speare.lt>*. Beautiful and comfortable, Sonnets, inside the Shakespeare Boutique Hotel *(see page 131)*, is one of the most expensive restaurants in Vilnius and definitely a cut above the rest. Walls are painted a comforting deep red and the menu is guaranteed to transport you to a place of culinary delight. Most major credit cards accepted.

Stikliai €€€€€ *Gaono 7; tel: 264 95 80*. The Stikiliai group owns a hotel *(see page 131)* and numerous cafés and restaurants across the city, and this restaurant is the spectacular dénouement of their success story. The skilful fusion of Lithuanian and French cuisine puts this restaurant on a par with establishments in large cities far from this little Baltic capital. Definitely for the well-heeled and those who must entertain them, or for a special night out. Open daily noon–midnight. Most major credit cards accepted. Next door is the old-fashioned and upmarket beer cellar, Stiklių Aludė, which serves more traditional fare for a third of the price. Open daily noon–midnight. Most major credit cards accepted.

Tores €€–€€€ *Užupio 40; tel: 262 93 09*. This place has the best outdoor seating in the entire city. Overlooking the Old Town, the terrace here is the place to be during the warmer months. In winter the windows ensure a good view of a rainy or snowy cityscape. Food is unbeatably charming if a bit on the basic side. The menu is mostly Lithuanian, even though they tout themselves as lovers of Spanish wines (hence the name), with a few international dishes. Reservations are usually essential, especially in summer. Open Mon–Thur, Sun 11am–midnight, Fri–Sat 11am–2am. Most major credit cards accepted.

Žemaičių Smuklė €€€ *Vokiečių 24; tel: 261 65 73*. Set in an atmospheric collection of cellar rooms, this is quite possibly the most rollicking place in Vilnius in which to sample the local cuis-ine. Although the prices here seem to be going up along with the restaurant's reputation, the food is still good value. Quite a few vegetarian options are available for those who don't mind choos-ing from various potato dishes. The courtyard provides outdoor seating during the warmer months. The home-made beer is potent and thirst-quenching. Open 11am–midnight. Most major credit cards accepted.

CITY CENTRE

Avilys €€ *Gedimino 5; tel: 212 19 00; <www.avilys.lt>.* A variety of beers are brewed on the premises and leaving without tasting one is close to reprehensible. The menu has a variety of grilled meat dishes. Open daily 11am–1am. Most major credit cards accepted.

Čagino €€ *Basanavičiaus 11; tel: 261 55 55.* By far the best option for Russian food in the centre of the city should you want to tuck into a cuisine that's similar but still different from the Lithuanian. Occasionally, boisterous groups of Russian men swilling vodka take over part of the restaurant, but the worst they'll do is sing off-key. Open daily noon–midnight. Most major credit cards accepted.

Neringa €€€ *Gedimino 23; tel: 261 40 58.* Now one of the eateries in the Scandic Neringa Hotel *(see page 134)*, the Neringa restaurant during Soviet times was the stamping ground of the Communist elite. Today, the interior murals are a reminder of the hard-working peasants and the regimented side of socialism. For authenticity order the chicken Kiev, for which they are known. Weekend live music performances get the middle-aged crowd on to the dance floor at the centre of the dining room. Open Mon–Wed, Sun 9am–11pm, Thur–Sat 9am–midnight. Most major credit cards accepted.

Prie Parlamento €€ *Gedimino 46; tel: 249 66 06.* A staple of expat life in Vilnius is this British-owned restaurant/bar/nightclub across the street from the Parliament building. Catering for travellers in town for a few days to a few years, the menu has basic staples such as pasta, as well as a few more inspiring dishes such as the seafood dishes. Both the ground floor and second floor serve food; the upper floor has a more subdued ambiance. Open Mon–Wed 10am–3am, Fri–Sat 10am–5pm, Sun 10am–2am. Most major credit cards accepted.

Ukrainos Vakarai €€ *Algirdo 5; tel: 265 03 02.* Although the decor and cuisine may be similar to many other restaurants in the city, the ear will no doubt pick up the thumping sound of Ukrainian pop music that fills the place. The downstairs cellar is far more charming than the upstairs area. Garlic and vodka are the primary staples so you'll come out happy but smelling nothing like roses. Located up the hill of Basanavičiaus Street just a few metres from the Old Town. Open Mon–Thur 11am–10pm, Fri–Sat noon–midnight, Sun noon–11pm. Most major credit cards accepted.

Užupio Picerija €–€€ *Paupio 3; tel: 215 36 66.* The place is small so expect to wait during busier times or to share a table with other diners. The pizza is of the popular, thin-crust variety. Nice touches and attention to detail – the spicy pizza is actually spicy – make this a decent option for those in the Užupis area. Open daily 8am–11pm.

FURTHER AFIELD

Riverside Restaurant €€€€ *Konstitucijos 20; tel: 272 62 72.* Tucked inside the Reval Hotel *(see page 134)*, this restaurant is remarkable in the way that its chefs demonstrate a respect for food often found lacking in many of the city's other restaurants. The light flavours of fish, for example, are allowed to come through rather than be overwhelmed by heavy sauces. Expect an excellent meal. Open Mon–Fri 6.30am–11.30pm, Sat–Sun 7am–11.30pm. Most major credit cards accepted.

Vandens Malūnas €€–€€€ *Verkių 100; tel: 271 16 66; <www.vandensmalunas.lt>.* The terrace of Vandens Malūnas (the Water Mill) is one of Vilnius' best summer afternoon spots, especially for those with children. Located a few kilometres north of the central area (and only easily reached by car or taxi), the restaurant is inside what used to be a working mill. The menu runs the gamut of fish and meat dishes. The vegetarian options and children's menu, though small, are well chosen. In winter the action takes place in the interior with its numerous rooms; some have fireplaces. Open daily 11.30am–midnight. Most major credit cards accepted.

INDEX